Damn the Diets

Why "Clean Eating" Failed You, How Fad Diets Destroy
Your Life and What to Do to Recover.

Kayla Rose Kotecki

Damn The Diets

DISCLAIMER

The success of your recovery is up to you, your commitment, your consistency, and your actions. By reading my books, enrolling in any of my courses, or signing up for consulting sessions with me, you are only guaranteed the success of that which you take and fully implement into your life. Always perform your own due diligence and use your own best judgment, following your intuitive sense on any decisions you make for your health and life.

The information in this book is based on my experience, research, and insight from others who have been through similar situations. It is not intended as a substitute for the advice of your doctor. The reader should regularly consult a physician, therapist, or counselor in matters relating to his/ her physical or mental health, particularly regarding any symptoms that may require diagnosis or medical attention. If you use any of the information in this book, the author and the publisher assume no responsibility for your actions.

DamnTheDiets.com/home

Want 3 free guides that accompany this book?

Head over to:

DamnTheDiets.com

And enter your email to receive some exclusive *free* goods I've put together for you as an extension to this book.

Enjoy :)

TABLE OF CONTENTS

LETS CALL THIS CHAPTER ONE...

Have you embarked on few or many diets in the past, all of which restricted something (calories, whole food groups) or are ingrained in one diet or diet ideology?

Did you, whilst in the pursuit to "be the healthiest you could be," *lose* a lot of the health you still had to start with?

Have you been stuck in a diet prison such as: The Fitness Model and Bodybuilding Competitor lifestyle, Raw Veganism, Fruitarianism, Ketogenic, Atkins, Paleo, Whole30, or anything else that is oppressively restrictive?

Have you noticed you've lost your sanity, social and personal life, mental/physical/emotional health, and/or passion for life due to restrictive behaviors, dieting, and lifestyle habits? Is it because you have invested too much energy into a diet/dogma, trying to live up to societal pressures to look a certain way or eat a certain way?

Have you lost touch with your intuition and satiety/hunger signals after following different "health gurus," the health and fitness industry guidelines, or any other restrictive diets or dogmas?

Are you sick of living in a restrictive prison that sucks the life, joy, and health from you and now want to reclaim your life, health, relationships, passion, and "jolly joy"?

Unfortunately, at one point, I was in a place where I answered yes to all the above questions, but I could transform from full denial into true recovery, reclaiming all these losses and more. Now, it's my responsibility to share with whomever will listen, take responsibility, and take action, what I did to heal. Hear that? Take Action. Yep, I'm one of those action freaks. Because it's the only way to succeed and achieve what you truly desire, in any area of your life, recovery included. Sitting on that beautiful butt of yours, hoping everything will fall into place and into your lap is a fairytale dream, not the reality we live in. So, you got to take action, Tony Robbins style.

Are you open to the idea that dieting, restricting, starving, over exercising, being too rigid, and whatever else you're into is harmful to your health and wellbeing, and you now need to "recover" from the mental and physical damage done? Do you still want to be healthy, without having to be locked up in your isolated dieting-dogma-ditch of perfection? Do you want this, combined with the mental freedom not to have a panic attack if all doesn't go as planned? Do you want to have a healthy relationship with food, exercise, and yourself?

My goal is to help people break free from restrictive dieting, anorexia, and the average yo-yo dieting or your "fad-trend diet" followers. I want to help guide people back from the mental and physical damage and programming done from the media, modern society, the health and fitness industry, and other various popular "fad" diet trends. I want to help people to get their priorities straight.

I stand against rules, restrictions, unquestionable guidelines, and forbidden foods/ behaviors /thoughts around food, exercise, self-love, and things of that nature. I stand against not listening to your own intuition and putting your trust into someone else outside of yourself. I stand against the sacrificing of internal health and feelings of a healthy body/mind/soul, to place external appearance above all.

Life is more than looking picture perfect, obsessing around diet, and being fearful or anxious regarding weight, appearance, and adherence of nutritional dogmas. I know how daunting, life-sucking, and energy zapping these rules in life can be. Everywhere we turn, we face the societal pressures to live up to these unrealistic body standards and expectations. Living only to maintain the superficial takes the fun, joy, and passion out of your life. Even if not right away, slowly over time, more of life's pleasures fade away.

Have you ever compared those who are into drugs, drinking, smoking, fast food/processed food, or other behaviors of self-harm and unhealthful living with those striving to be super "pure" and ultra-healthy, the models or actors who look "perfect" on the magazine ads, social media #fitspo accounts, or movie screens? The ones always searching for the next health trend, magic pill, or exercise routine that will shed pounds in a matter of a couple days, or how about the ones dedicated to following any other "perfect" diet, lifestyle, or health guru? Haven't you noticed... these people following some or all these things, seem to be the ones who are facing the most health struggles? They often are the most unhealthful, uptight, closed off, irritable, lonely, depressed, non-joyful, low libido people out of the general populace. I'm talking about the groups of folks who are Low-Carb'ers (Ketogenic/Atkins), Vegans/Raw Vegans, Weight Watchers, South Beach Diet, High-Carb Low-Fat, "eat less to live longer," Orthorexic, bodybuilder/ bikini competitors/fitness models diet, extreme athletes that develop an eating disorder... the list goes on.

I know these people, because I was once one of them. The word miserable comes to mind. These are the people who decided to throw out their intuition and listen to an outside source or diet plan that has no true idea what each body truly needs. These folks, myself at one point and maybe you, rely on "willpower," listening to the vague and impersonal mathematical equations that dictate our eating and lifestyle habits, despite our body's unique needs. We suppress the *gift* of hunger and satiety signals our body uses as a communication tool to us. We think our minds can outsmart our intelligent bodies, even when our bodies do all the work automatically behind the scenes, and we have no involvement besides putting the foods into our mouths, chewing, and swallowing when cued to. We push our bodies into semi-starvation or take it further into full blown starvation, and we watch our health crumble to pieces, and our lives become dull, lethargic, and spiritless.

No amount of willpower, self-control, any specific diet, or way of eating will ever fix this problem of obsessing around food or fearing food. This is more of a mental problem and the mindset you have set around eating and your body image. Trying to fix this problem with more self-control or by trying to find the "perfect diet" is only a setup for disappointment, leaving you frustrated with yourself and food.

A "diet" just doesn't work; a diet isn't limited to the actions of going on Weight Watchers, Atkins, or Raw Vegan/Fruitarian. A diet is a way of eating you are emotionally attached to. This means you think: "If I eat this certain way, I'm alright, but if I don't eat this way, I'm miserable, I'm lazy, I'm unworthy, I'm a failure, and I will beat myself up for it." Whenever we feel guilt or shame with our choices around food, when we cross these boundaries we set for ourselves of being "alright," we send our body the message, "our diet is going to start tomorrow. I better get everything I can in now." You binge and perhaps purge. You keep telling yourself "tomorrow will be the day I start, or Monday, or next week," and keep with the diet. You stress yourself out unnecessarily with these thoughts. You think everything will be perfect, you'll be happier, you'll finally love yourself, you'll finally be good enough, you'll finally be able to enjoy life in a new way... but guess what...that day never comes. It'll always be the second Tuesday of next week. Even if you get yourself to lose enough weight from extended restriction, you still feel none of these good feelings you expected to. It's never good enough. So, you keep pushing yourself.

All these diet trend wars out there are each claiming to be the *perfect one* and the only way to health, healing, and ideal weight. Yet in every group, there's both success and failure, so how could only one specific diet be for everyone? These restrictive diet trends (as in, restricting some form of food, caloric intake, etc.) are all ultimately very unbalanced. After the initial so-called "benefits," a dieter will run into some major and detrimental problems, physically, mentally, or both. These diets instill fear in you for whatever the "fear food" or "food groups" in each trend are; the claims are that the foods are "poison, evil, and addictive," and they must be avoided for true and optimal health. Undoubtedly, when one embarks on a restrictive diet, one sees previous inexperienced issues popping up or becoming exacerbated, including digestive troubles, autoimmune reactions, constipation, food allergies, irritability, fatigue, obsessiveness, anxieties, imbalanced hormones, lowered metabolism, loss of libido, loss of menses, and more.

You may not yet believe it's possible for you to recover because of *your* situation, being in the mental and physical state you're in... But, it's staying OPEN to new ideas, and as the path is shown to you along the way, something might click for you, and your whole perspective will change for the better. This will be just the beginning of your road to restriction recovery. Allow yourself to dream without limits, no matter how far gone or in-deep you think you are. There is always a way out, and there is always hope; empower yourself to this thought.

Ask yourself what is blocking you from taking on full recovery. Get to the core. There is always a root cause of where, when, and why it all started for you. This can be a mental illness of disordered eating, an unhealthy relationship with food and with yourself, fear of weight gain, or fear that others won't approve, keeping you from living a normal and pleasurable life! Don't you want to become empowered and refuse to allow a restrictive eating disorder (or anything in that matter) defeat you and take away anymore of your life than it already has?

Let go of toxic control to regain healthy control. You are NOT losing control when you go into recovery; you will regain control over your life as you heal and defeat the DE (disordered eating) demons. Stop these disordered thoughts and beliefs from controlling every aspect of your valuable life! Your DE will scream when it's threatened in recovery, but don't let that DE tantrum get its way anymore. It needs a permanent time-out.

What if the goal wasn't to stick to your diet anymore against your bodily requests to eat those "fear foods" you have off limits? What if the goal was to eat with peace, love, normalcy, and sanity? It's time to change your goals around how you deal with food.

I used to be in a place, like I assume you are, constantly reading blogs and forums and listening to videos all over the internet, YouTube, Facebook, Instagram, etc. I would impulsively get and read every book I could land my hands on and spend thousands of dollars on doctor visits and coaching sessions in pursuit of the "perfect, most healthful, diet." It's sad that people with good intentions in adopting a health-promoting practice can end up creating more personal harm than existed in the first place. They're trying their hardest with all their efforts and dedication, but somehow only getting worse. This happened to me; maybe it happened to you.

If an eating disorder is not caused from genetic mental illness, then most eating disorders can, and do, start from diets and the desire to be "healthier or slimmer." Just a simple diet wanting to lose weight, or eat healthy, or get fit can devolve into a full-blown eating disorder right under one's nose. Engaging in a restrictive diet can lead to bulimia, the binge-purge-cycle, extreme body dysmorphia, anorexia, over-exercising (another form of purging), the obsessiveness to eat only "clean and pure" foods, the stress and anxiety to measure and weigh all your foods, or all the other disordered behaviors that develop.

There are people with eating disorders that don't have body dysmorphia problems; they really think they're just wanting to be "healthier," but can still fall into a full-blown eating disorder. Others who have body dysmorphia (which most with DE's do) become so used to seeing their weak and fragile self, or the way they imagine their "ideal body," that they think they appear normal. Being in this state makes it even harder to come out of the eating disorder mentality or even to realize one has a problem.

We are brainwashed into thinking our body can't maintain a healthy weight without calorie counting/restricting and over-exercising, and thinking we must restrict certain foods or we become "addicted" and over-eat them. We are encouraged to believe we must always exercise more and eat less or think we overeat *only* because of emotional issues.

We are taught to feel guilt and shame if we eat more than the recommended guideline as to what we should eat for body weight(numbers), BMI (numbers), height (numbers), age(numbers), calories(numbers), at a certain time (numbers), our clothing sizes (numbers)- we are living for NUMBERS. Our bodies are more intelligent and intuitive than what these numbers can give and tell us. Yet, we allow these numbers to dictate our lives, thoughts, and actions, even though these numbers are so generalized, they don't (and can't) consider the other many crucial factors (environmental, stress, activity level, metabolism, genetic, etc.) that individually affect us all and our normal eating actions.

"How is it that most peoples' body fat mass stays relatively stable over long periods of time when an imbalance of as little as 5% of calories should lead to rapid changes in weight? Is it because we do complicated calculations in our heads every day, factoring in basal metabolic rate and exercise, to make sure our energy intake precisely matches expenditure? Of course not. We're gifted with a sophisticated system of hormones and brain regions that do the "calculations" for us unconsciously. When it's working properly, this system precisely matches energy intake to expenditure, ensuring a stable and healthy fat mass. It does this by controlling food seeking behaviors, feelings of fullness and even energy expenditure by heat production and physical movements. If you eat a little bit more than usual at a meal, a properly functioning system will say "let's eat a little bit less next time, and perhaps also burn some of it off." This is one reason why animals in their natural habitat are nearly always at an appropriate weight, barring starvation. The only time wild animals are overweight enough to significantly compromise physical performance is when it serves an important purpose, such as preparing for hibernation" (Stephan Guyenet, Whole Health Resource).

8

We are so brainwashed by the media, the numbers, the health guidelines out there today, and so many other factors that we've forgotten how to trust and listen to our own bodies! Our brilliant bodies know best; heck, they're doing all the nitty gritty work behind the scenes without us even realizing it most of the time (hormone production, the transformation of oxygen into carbon dioxide, every enzymatic function in the body, heart beating, every organ function, digestion of food, ATP production, I mean the list is too long to go on). We often take every little action for granted and are very unappreciative, yet we think WE can dictate and know what our body needs? Preposterous, I tell ya!

We are constantly told messages like "the fat you eat is the fat you wear," or "carbs make you fat," or "we really don't need to eat that much," or "you must have a parasite if you have any cravings," or "your body lies to you." We are presented with magical diets and weight loss pills that claim to give us results in a fraction of the time that it would naturally (and healthfully) take. Yes, you may get quick results with all these diets and magic potions, but in the long term, you only set yourself up for binging, gaining more weight than you had before, and chronic health problems, such as hormonal, digestive, kidney and heart problems, dependency on the pills/leader, etc. It's just not worth it. You will just make yourself sick, miserable, and unhealthy. That is not a life worth living.

If the fad diets and magic weight loss pills worked, everybody wouldn't still be struggling with weight and would be in perfect health. Everybody would be at their ideal weight, perfect, happy, zippity-doo-dah's, and nobody would keep yo-yo dieting or be on the continual quest for the next best diet trend/pill! The weight loss industry would lose too much money if it all worked permanently; it keeps us stuck, dependent, always searching for and BUYING the next best magic trick or pill. If you cannot sustain the diet and restrictions forever without facing health problems, then it should not even be done for a week, month, or a year. A healthy diet is one you can do indefinitely, easily, and pleasurably, with no negative side effects.

Daily, we are exposed to unrealistic ideal body types on YouTube, Instagram, Facebook, Snapchat, magazines, TV, movies, and billboards. How can we not eventually develop some kind of insecurity as to how we look? I mean, we are constantly bombarded with these subliminal and rather blunt messages as to how we should look, act, talk, do, and aspire for. How can we blame the majority of the population for feeling insecure, not good enough, and feeling the need to conform? How can we look down upon people who develop eating disorders and see them as weak or crazy? Those that suffer from an ED are just trying to live up to these harsh and unrealistic demands and expectations of society and the media, demands at an ever-increasing rate in today's age. We have been taught to believe, since a young age and daily, what "beauty" is, what "success" is, what's good, what's bad, what's "cool," what's "weird," what's acceptable, what's to be silenced, and what it looks like to be "healthy." While beauty standards have always been a part of our culture, the inundation of exposure to these arbitrary and unrealistic standards did not exist in the past the way it does today.

Diets are focused on restriction and deprivation. Dieting makes it easier to fall into a pattern of disordered eating. Dieting is not a long-term solution. Dieting distorts our self-image. Diets often cause people to put all their self-worth into the way their body looks or how much they weigh. It is all too easy to compare one's own body to those of photoshopped celebrities and models on magazine covers, and people become critical of themselves, their bodies, their eating choices, their thought patterns, and their exercise regimes. Instead of always trying to alter your body, looks, diet, or exercise regime, first, try to alter your distorted mindset towards your body and self that's been learned from modern day diet culture that's driving all the dysfunctional behaviors.

What's shown to us through the media does not reflect the real factors that took place to manipulate the photos/Ads/posts. A lot of what we see and aspire towards is nowhere near real, and if it is real, if they are as skinny or ripped as they are, then they are living in a hellhole of a prison. I've been there, and that's the best way to describe what it's like to prep for photoshoots, fitness competitions, Instagram photos, dieting down, dehydrating yourself — I felt like a walking corpse with death itself near my side. The photos are then photoshopped, edited, filtered, air brushed, touched up, provided specific lighting, certain poses, particular angles, slabbed with Johnson's baby oil, sprayed with artificial and toxic tanners, caked with layers of makeup. All of this and more comes into play to make the perfect photo. You can see the same person on the same day from a photoshoot, and they look nothing like what they look like in the photo. So, the people in the photos don't even look that way, yet we, the general population, are supposed to attain that ideal ourselves?! Get the point of how crazy this all is yet?! This is not glamorous, but ludicrous.

I am definitely not against social media or media. The media can and should be used for people's benefit, yet observations of it often result in negativity and detriment to one's psyche.

There are a lot of silent sufferers out there that are afraid to admit or talk to anyone about that fact they are always concerned about these topics. There are other people always thinking about food, exercise, body flaws — I again, was one of them. I was in denial, complete and utter denial. It's pretty dang embarrassing looking back. I did not want to talk about what I was feeling and the frustration and confusion I was dealing with. I did not want to show weakness or vulnerability. I wanted to do it all on my own. I thought I could do everything all by myself. I wanted people to only see a fake facade of what my life was. What a joke!

If you look at the way Nature works — everything, everyone, from the ants, to the wind, to the oxygen, to the birds, to each of the plants, to each of the animals — we're all interconnected. We all help each other, directly or indirectly, living symbiotically together (or *should* be) whether we're aware of it or not. Accept help when you need it. Don't go about life alone, doing everything on your own. You are only hurting yourself, and preventing, or rather, stunting, your growth. If you are appreciative with good intentions when you receive any help, it's different than receiving help with entitlement and expectations. This was the best realization I could have experienced for my recovery and growth as a person and in life, becoming open to help from others and new ways of doing things, approaching things, and thinking of things.

Realize all the superficial and materialistic things *we think* matter to us *now* will *not* matter to us later in life, or after we pass (hate to break it to you, but we don't get out of this life alive, if you weren't aware). We don't leave life with our material items and our stick-thin starved physical body. These things just don't matter! We are focusing (and wasting) our precious energy in the wrong ways if we are living for only external sources of happiness and ways to fill our voids for self-worth and happiness. This couldn't be farther from what truly will satisfy our spiritual, emotional, mental, and physical needs. It's okay to want to look good, be clean, and feel/look healthy and attractive. Of course!

But when we base our whole life, with an extreme demand to be perfect, it makes life a living hell. Plus, attractive, clean, healthy, pretty, handsome is all relative to each beholder. One word: Balance. Find Balance!

A nurse friend I have works in the hospital and has dealt with many people on their deathbeds. What was their top regret if they had any? What matters most to people on their death bed? She told me they care most about how and if they lived their life, if they lived life to the fullest every day, and if they were a good human being. They wished they didn't waste their time being insecure, or isolated, or striving after material goods. Nothing about looking perfect or living up to the trends was something they wished they would have focused their energy on. That stuff is meaningless; when you're faced with reality and the reality of death, you're forced to reflect on the real purpose of what life is about.

My mom, who is also a wonderful and respected nurse, has worked in multiple hospitals throughout her career. She told me she'll never forget what her patients shared with her when they were diagnosed with serious diseases or were terminally ill. Their priorities totally change; what truly matters is spending time with the ones you love. The things they worried about just the day before, such as bills, paperwork, money, "things," or the worries of life, they now had no care in the world for. She told me about Erik Erickson's - *Stages of old age,* which is: *"You're either going to look back on your life with integrity, or despair/regret."* What do you want?

Think about the 18/40/60 rule. This stands for, *"When you are 18, you worry about what everyone thinks of you, when you are age 40 you don't give a damn what anyone thinks about you, and when you're age 60, you realize no one has been thinking about you at all. People spend their days worrying and thinking about themselves; you don't have to"* (Dr Amen M.D., Change Your Brain Change Your Life). Live for yourself, not others. Screw other people! Okay, I'm joking, we are social beings when it comes down to it, and it's nice to be loved by others, but we shouldn't solely base our actions and lifestyle decisions in hopes to be approved and loved by others nor to fit in to society just to get by.

Please read through this book, with an open heart and mind, and go with how you feel deep inside. Listen more to how your heart is reacting and focus less on how your mind/ego is reacting, but also find a balance between the mind and heart. I wrote this text for those who I feel so deeply for, struggling for their health, trapped in an eating disorder prison. Why? Because I've been there too.

All phases of my eating disorder stole a big chunk of my life. I went through anorexia, bulimia, over-exercising, re-stricting (foods, calories, and times to eat), and orthorexia. I was just trying to be "healthy," or so I thought, and want-ed to "do the best I could," to be the healthiest I could be. It all sucked the energy, happiness, joy, and health right out of me.

It ruined my close and dear relationships, stopped me from living life to the fullest and experiencing opportuni-ties I could have otherwise. Yet, I don't regret one mo-ment, because I feel stronger than I ever have in my life after what I've went through, and the whole journey gave me a driving passion and renowned purpose. I now want to share with others to help them (you) to break free from this prison. I got out of this sickness with a strong deter-mination to raise awareness and spread the insight I gath-ered along my healing journey to help all who are suffer-ing, but who also have the desire and willingness to re-claim their life/health.

If you're feeling stuck, and you don't know where to turn or where to start, but know you want to get your life back and stop living in a disordered and restrictive lifestyle, this is a great book (I'm totally not being biased at all) to help guide you! In this book, I am going to show you all I know on how to become your own boss again so you don't have to rely on any outside source, guru, coach, etc., on what to eat, when to eat, how much to eat, or why to eat.

UNDERSTANDING RESTRICTIVE EATING AND RECOVERY

A restrictive Eating disorder is best described as the misidentification in the brain of food as a threat. It is defined as mental illness within the Diagnostic and Statistical Manual of Mental Illness (DSM). (EDInstitue.org) *extreme dietary restraint and restriction, binge eating, self-induced vomiting and the misuse of laxatives, driven exercising, body checking and avoidance, and the over-evaluation of control over eating, shape and weight.* Eating Disorders are mental illnesses with biological *and* environmental causes.

Eating disorders are not just the restriction of calories, but also restricting the *types* of foods; this form of disordered eating is also known as the relatively new phenomena Orthorexia. Yet, people that are orthorexic will immediately write that classification off as absurd, foolish, irrational, and laughable (I was there, so pissed they even came out with a diagnosis for people, including myself, that were just trying *to be healthy*). This is a real and serious ED that obsessively restricts whole food groups. These food groups are not to be feared, but are healthy and important aspects to our diet; they have been included around the world, in almost all cultures, for hundreds of thousands of years without question.

Let's get clear on the following factors, so you can connect the dots as we continue forth in this book... Low- this or Low- that in a diet is an eating disorder (such as HCLF-

High Carb Low Fat, or HFLC- High Fat Low Carb or High Protein Low Fat and the like). Raw foodism/fruitarianism is an eating disorder (disordered behaviors around eating). Low calorie diets, less than 2,000 calories a day is an eating disorder. Cutting out or severely limiting whole food groups such as starchy carbs, saturated fat, sugar or any other staple energy source for humans, is an eating disorder. Abusing fasting (water, juice, and/or dry) and cleanses for any reason, is an eating disorder. Consistently skipping meals on purpose despite your hunger cues is an eating disorder. Feeling fear, shame, and anxiety around food is an eating disorder. Manipulating and abusing your diet, exercise, body, and supplements/pills in ways that are not sustainable nor healthy for the long term is an eating disorder.

You get the hint; all of these trendy diets, dogmas, and "lifestyles" floating around today, are disordered behaviors around food and eating. The question is, to what extent do you take these set rules and guidelines? While many aren't extremists, there are a lot of individuals who are and take these suggestions to unhealthy measures. The first step to recovery, is admitting there's a problem within your restrictive or obsessive routine, and coming out of denial. The next is to take responsibility and take actions towards changing these negative habits, beliefs, and behaviors. Hey, we're not in Alcoholics Anonymous here, but we could call it Extremist Dieters Anonymous or Body Shaming Anonymous if we wanted to.

People with long-term intractable eating disorders, the anxiety surrounding the impact of an eating disorder, reinforces a desire to avoid thinking about its impact on your health. It's easier to be worried that the symptoms are not responsible for the eating disorder than to consider the possibility that the eating disorder is really to blame.

Recovery is made of a bunch of steps forward, and maybe a step back or a setback, without reverting to your old ways and restricting food, over exercising, purging, etc. Recovery is a process that takes a lot of work, mentally and physically. You CAN do it. I believe in you, I know you're worth it, I know you're capable, and I know you're better than the eating disorder. Remember, there's no quick fix to TRUE authentic health and healing, even if we are engulfed in the quick-fix, easy way out, pop a pill, codependent mentality of modern society.

The steps to follow and suggestions are consistent. Your situation is not different. There aren't exceptions for your case. You can't use the excuse, "Well, my situation is different than others with disordered eating because "blank" .... There are no reasons to justify why you think your situation is the exception. I was in denial for years, because I honestly thought I had no eating disorder; I was different because I was just being "healthy" and I was living on "the most optimal diet for human beings" and justifications like these, even though I looked like skin and bones and my health was falling apart and getting worse by the moment. I didn't just have everybody else around me convinced, but I had myself convinced.

The ED voice will tell you "oh, you're not *that* bad," or "you don't have an eating disorder!" If you're here in these pages, it's likely you have some sort of disordered eating. Whether it's from fitness bikini/figure competitions/training/modeling, or if it's from restrictive diets and dogmas out there these days (like raw vegan, ketogenic, high-protein, low-carb, grain-free, etc.), whatever level or areas you've been at, there are many faces and practices of disordered eating behaviors. Yeah, you may get short term results with any of these diets, but in the long term, you'll most definitely ruin your hormones, mood, endocrine glands, digestive capabilities, and lower and impair your metabolism.

The fact that you're reading this book is a good and sure sign you are seeking help, guidance, change and support, which is the first and most important step for recovery. There is a reason you are searching for answers, and why you were led to this very book. If you're here, you're facing some problem from disordered eating and searching for answers and needing to make a change for your health's sake. Basically, in a social dynamic perspective, you (consciously or unconsciously) came to these pages with some level of insecurity about what you are doing in terms of 'detoxing,' cleansing, restricting or dieting.

Your openness to listen to my insight and read what I have to share shows your desire to grow and expand your knowledge. It shows your aptitude for being open-minded and accepting new ways and approaches, and the strength and courage to question your current beliefs and ways of living that have *not* been working in your favor...

You need to take back the reins, and no longer allow the ED to obstruct your health and happiness. It's time to take full responsibility: you have poor heath because you have an eating disorder. It's time to come up from beneath the clouds of denial and wake up to reality. Life is calling, so stop ignoring it.

To achieve full recovery, or any steps towards recovery, you must commit 110%. No half-assing recovery, you got to whole-ass this task. Nobody else can do the work for you; this is all a battle your own. It's a battle between YOU, your mind, your belief system, your conditioned and manipulated thoughts (by society and you), your body, and your Eating Disorder's ego. Other people can support your recovery process and hold you accountable, but nobody can face your ED demons and overcome them, nobody but you.

There is no helping someone not yet ready to commit or change themselves; you probably know that by now. But when a person is ready, and they want it enough, I'm here, your loved ones are there, and many other recovery warriors are out there to help others get through this battle.

Here's an excerpt from (Oras, Elisa. BrainwashED):

"Here's an example of how dieting leads to eating disorders: First, you have a goal to lose weight or get "trim, toned, and sexy."

Or maybe you just want to eat "healthy" and give up a lot of the "unhealthy" foods you love. You start to diet – you restrict foods and/ or calories.

You hashtag #finallygettinghealthy on your protein shake Instagram picture. Initially, you lose weight, and you think… Amazzzing!! Finally! #thingsarehappening…

But then you start to have cravings. At first, you resist the urge and use your willpower to avoid eating and stick to your diet. But sooner or later, you give in. You binge. You overeat. You let go of the restriction and say the hell with it! You eat everything you have been restricting.

After the binge, when you begin to think clearly again and come out of your food coma, you realize what you have done. You have "ruined" your diet. Your life is basically over. You get upset, feel panicky and out of control, and can FEEL how you are getting fatter by the minute. You feel fear and disgust. You feel like you've become this dangerous, insatiable, eat-everything-on-this-planet kind of Foodzilla who has to be stopped.

After this, you promise yourself to be a "good girl/ boy" tomorrow and start over. But today? Well, you've already blown it, so you might as well eat for the rest of the day...

The next day you start to restrict and diet again, but this time with even more fear and obsession. You want to be sure that yesterday's binge never happens again... and the monster is stopped from doing any further damage to the world's food storage...

But eventually, the same thing happens – you feel the urge to eat more than allowed and the kind of foods that are forbidden on your diet. And eventually, you binge again. You have now entered dieting merry-go-hell.

Of course, thanks to dieting, your metabolism is much slower now, and you've also lost quite an amount of muscle and water weight thanks to restriction. You've lost some digestive enzymes and might find it very hard to digest some of the foods you formerly ate, causing you to get easily bloated and constipated.

So now when you start to eat more – or even normal amounts of foods – you gain weight very quickly. You can gain all the weight back, often times weighing even more than you did originally. You may find it very hard to eat normal amounts and feel totally bloated after a meal.

Welcome, ladies and gents! You are now trapped in a vicious cycle of yo-yo dieting! You have been brainwashed to believe you just need more willpower to continue dieting and it's all your fault it didn't work.

Some stop here and give up dieting (or become chronic yo-yo dieters)...

But some continue with extreme measures to get rid of the weight "once and for all" – welcome, eating disorder!

Some people begin to overeat uncontrollably (binge eating), some binge and purge (bulimia), some starve themselves (anorexia), some obsessively avoid particular foods (orthorexia), some overexercise (bulimia or anorexia athletica), and some may have all of these together (EDNOS – eating disorder not otherwise specified)."

This sounded like my second wave (out of my 4) of my new eating disorder. It's all too common these days scrolling through social media outlets daily. Dieting can be one of the primary triggers leading to an eating disorder; getting rid of the dieting could wipe out 70% of eating disorders, according to YMCA Reflections on Body Image, online magazine, Kathy A. Benedetto, and Stephen Todd Callahan, MD.

Healing is not something fun to endure, but it is worth it. Don't expect recovery to be painless. Honestly, recovery can be heart wrenching, physically daunting, distressing, full of body aches and pains, fatigue after eating, uncontrollable binges and extreme hunger, brain fog, headaches, digestive discomforts, mood swings, edema, swelling, and heartburn. Things will be amplified if you are coming from a fruitarian or raw vegan diet, severely low-calorie diet, or a low-carb diet. You may feel as if every food is killing you or making you sicker, as if the foods are poisoning your bloodstream and body, wrecking your brain or destroying your nervous system.

But as you continue, you WILL see improvements. You will get glimpses of energy, a state of calmness, states of bliss, a desire to reconnect with past relationships, feelings of sexual desire, an inner growing strength, greater aptitude to handle many foods and more. You'll come alive again.

You'll understand this feeling as you feel it, as it is hard to grasp at first that it can ever happen to you in the state you're in. I never believed it would happen for me. I couldn't see the light until it showed up randomly as I continued to take action towards recovery. Don't worry. I had the same doubts initially, but the healing happened and even surpassed my expectations.

I know the darkness disordered eating brings and all the life it takes away from us. I went through my recovery journey alone, so I want to make sure others with the desire to recover won't be alone. I want to help show you what to do, and what not to do...so you can get it right the first time and set yourself up for success. I want to be the support I wish I had and to help be your mirror, so you can see how valuable you are and how worth it you are to recover. Having healthy self-esteem is believing you are worth working in your own best interest.

The only way out of an eating disorder is to EAT. Yes, it's that simple. You need to keep eating, even when you feel ill, when you feel achy, and when you feel like giving up altogether. The only way to come over the ill symptoms is to keep eating. Watch your body strengthen and adapt. The more you eat, the more your body will strengthen, and the better you'll be able to handle food again.

"High frequency of dieting (rather than dieting per se) and earlier dieting onset were associated with poorer physical and mental health (including depression), more disordered eating (bingeing and purging), extreme weight and shape dissatisfaction and more frequent general health problems. The results suggest that there is a need for programs that will enhance self-esteem and weight/ shape acceptance and promote more appropriate

strategies for maintenance of healthy weight." (European Eating Disorders Review)

"Yo-yo dieting increases your risk of heart attack, stroke, diabetes, high blood pressure, cancer, immune system failure, impaired cognitive function, chronic fatigue, depression, and again... eating disorders." (Bailor, Jonathan. A Calorie Myth)

Dieting prior to or during pregnancy sets the kid up to have a higher chance for developing obesity and diabetes in today's modern diet. *"They made the rather startling discovery that adult children of mothers exposed to famine during the first two trimesters of their pregnancy were 80 percent more likely to be obese as adults... From this, the researchers theorized that deprivation in the first two trimesters primed these famine victims for a life of scarcity. When food became plentiful after the war, this 'thrifty fetus' effect backfired, with obesity as the consequence. Later, scientists would also note higher rates of heart disease, diabetes, and other chronic disease and even mental illness." (Ellen Ruppel Shell, The Hungry Gene)*

Have you ever noticed a super "fit" or very skinny mom and you noticed the kids to be more overweight than the rest of the kids their age, despite them being on the same "diet" as the "fit" mom? This study above may point at the contributing factors. When these kids become "fat" and not to their standard, the mom may become ashamed of the kid; the kid may be forced into weight loss programs, be made to feel awful and horrified, and be encouraged in many disordered eating behaviors, such as restrictive eating. What is lost on these parents is that restrictive eating behavior increases the chance of obesity later in adulthood more so than any known factor.

The elimination of dieting, restricting, and imposing beliefs to only attain one skinny body type can be the destruction of eating disorders. The rise of promotion of unrealistic body types from the media, social media, cultural expectations, and the general judgement of a superficial society has contributed to so many worldwide diet-induced eating disorders. You must realize restriction does not work and is not the answer. To recover, stop restricting altogether and forever from here on out. *"Trying to recover from an eating disorder while dieting is like trying to recover from a broken leg while still jumping on it.* (Oras, Elisa. BrainwashED) *There isn't a single peer-reviewed controlled clinical study of any weight-loss diet that shows success in significant weight loss over the long term. Not one. Remember what we said before? Diets have 99.5% failure rate! Most weight-loss diet studies are done a year or several years after the initial weight loss. Yes, calorie restriction may help you lose weight, BUT it's only temporary. You will gain the lost weight back in the following years, and that's if you're lucky – often you gain even more weight than you started with."*

WHAT DO YOU HAVE TO LOOK FORWARD TO IN RECOVERY?

When you recover, you WILL have quality of life without restrictions, limitations, cravings, moodiness, digestive problems, and bloating. You will get back your sex drive and menstrual cycle! You can regain all this without being underweight, overweight, moody, losing your hair, losing your sanity, losing your loved one, while taking back your quality of life. You won't be only obsessing about food, exercise, or body image 24/7 anymore. With this freed-up brain space, you'll be able to live life again. What do I mean by this? You'll be able to do and accomplish anything you desire. Everyone (yes, even you) has the power within to attain his or her biggest dreams; it just requires taking action!

You will have the desire to create new relationships outside of the home and internet and re-mend old relationships you may have lost during your eating disorder or pushed away if you self-isolated. You won't be an isolated hermit cave troll anymore (coined by my beloved brother, Robbie, lol!)

You can go back to work or school, because you now have the brain power and physical energy to sustain you and the desire to get back out in the world. You can heal the damage done to family relationships. You can beat insomnia and power through your day with sustained energy.

Your obsessive thoughts, behavior, and anxieties will diminish. You can go out all day and eat out along the way, without stressing about meals to prep beforehand, or making sure you'd be around some food when you're out or even calling restaurants or looking up the menu online ahead of time to make sure they are adequate for your restrictive diet preferences.

You won't feel stressed, instantly growing 20 gray hairs or crapping your pants, just because you try to leave the house or go to out in a social interaction. You can indulge in your favorite foods again without feeling guilty or ashamed. You won't feel the need to restrict, purge, or overexercise if you indulge in your favorite foods. You won't feel guilty if you go a couple days or weeks without exercising. You won't be secretly judging and feeling pissed about what others around you are eating.

You can go on vacations or trips away from the house or even go out for holiday dinners without obsessing about food. You'll be able to relax. You can laugh out loud. You will get your "jolly joy" back, and your passion and love for life will return.

You won't be trapped as a prisoner in your brain, fearful and not eating or nourishing your body, incessantly thinking about food and exercise. Your osteopenia and osteoporosis will reverse (may take up to 7 years for completion).

You will lose the desire and ability to binge! You'll have hunger cues guiding you when to eat, what to eat, and how much to eat, and you can follow those cues trustingly without guilt or restriction. You can feel satiety again and be a normal eater! You won't have to rely on "willpower" to refrain from overeating. Screw willpower! Bleh!

You will have an amped up healthy metabolism, which will support all around healthy bodily organ functions, hormone production, digestion, etc. You won't have digestive problems anymore; no more bloating, gas, stomach pains. You can maintain your weight effortlessly without dieting or over exercising!

You will get your period back and rebalance your hormones as you continue; I have no doubt! You are most likely underweight if you're reading this, and as you restore your weight and maintain the weight, it will come back. When malnourished, our body shuts off our fertility as it has to conserve for us to survive; it cannot take on another life form until it is healthy enough again. Your hair will stop falling out and grow back as lush as it was before, perhaps even more! The same goes for your nails, and they will stop being so brittle. Your skin will have a new glow to it.

These are just a few of the things I lost; you may have experienced some of these symptoms. You will regain lost parts of yourself though, so keep your eyes peeled as the carpet unfolds and you go along your recovery path. It is truly eye-opening once you experience it for yourself; only then can you get a genuine taste of what I'm trying to explain. It was magnificent how my eyes opened the more I progressed, and how much I realized *how deep I was in* and how much I had sacrificed and missed out on. In the beginning of recovery, I honestly rejected how deep I was into my ED. Heck, to be honest, I didn't think I had an Eating Disorder at all! I thought I was just your average "health seeker" and average dieter like everyone else. Wow, was I in denial!

I was bedridden, bloated, in pain, my whole body ached, brain fog, fatigued, zilch energy, anxious, irritable, fearful, unable to digest any foods anymore, had lost my menstrual cycle, was dizzy and faint, lost my sex drive, lost many relationships, lost my passion for life, isolated, my bones felt like they had osteoporosis, my nervous system felt like it was buzzing. It seemed body had developed many allergies and sensitivities to foods. I had night tremors, unable to sleep. I was severely underweight; my heart felt weak, and unsteady. I was constipated beyond belief. I relied on enemas daily for over a year, as well as laxatives and diuretics. I felt like binging when I would allow myself a fear food (which was rare). I had black outs and bouts of fainting. I felt disconnected and depressed; I was emotionally unstable and insecure. Thoughts about food were what my life consisted of, but the foods I craved were "feared and forbidden."

I didn't know if there was a light at the end of this tunnel I was in. I truly felt the foods must be toxic if I was feeling the way I was (nauseous, achy joints, painful feet and knees, edema, digestive discomfort, headaches, brain food, fatigue, etc.). I had been through 4 phases/kinds of restrictive eating disorders over the course of almost a decade, starting with anorexia in my teen years, leading to over exercising/fitness modeling/competing/restrictive dieting, which led to bulimia binge/purge, which then led to orthorexia.

Knowing and obsessing too much about "nutrition" ruined my life. It took away my life, and relationships, and freedom, and experiences, and fun, and happiness, and playfulness, and energy, and joy... It brought out qualities in me I never struggled with, such as the extremist tendencies, the obsessiveness and inflexibility, the loss of personality and crazy irritable/emotional rollercoaster, the complete pull away from loved ones and lack of intimacy. It made me never feel good enough and made me always seek to DO MORE, BE MORE, AND KNOW MORE... it made me feel superior and inflate my ego to unhealthy levels, thinking I was better than others who weren't AS health conscious or fit as I was or those within my community.

With all this information out there today, touting nutrition is the mother or all importantness (not a word, but now it is), yea maybe to an extent, it definitely matters, but nutrition overall should not be something we have to waste our life and every waking moment thinking about, or else we live (or not live) a miserable, dull, and isolated life. Think of health as being something that extends WAY beyond your diet. Your issue is not nutrition; it's more likely knowing *too much* about nutrition and having obsessive and disordered thoughts about your nutrition.

A main ingredient to my recovery protocol was, after I felt better and got my energy and life back, from just eating what I felt like guilt and fear free, I started going out and having fun again, laughing with old friends and family, having wine here and there, dancing, hiking, traveling, being less stressed, falling in love, sleeping, pursuing my passions, enjoying the simple pleasures of life, loving and accepting people for who they were, and all this made me so happy.

Feeling unsatisfied and shameful about my body and external appearance took away even more fun in my life and prevented me from taking up awesome opportunities and experiences with amazing people who wanted to share time with me and I with them. I couldn't come to terms with how I looked that day or month or year, and so I wouldn't allow myself to go out, in fear of judgment of others, and from myself. I limited myself and suppressed myself, and I see that happening within many people today.

Damn The Diets

The moment I cared TOO much about nutrition and body image, to impress a boy and others around me in society and live up to his and their standards and opinions, was the times I lost myself, my own opinions, my voice, and my drive. I lost myself in the attempt to please others. I lost my own self-love to gain others' love and approval.

Let me give you a summary of each of my phases, so you can better understand where I'm coming from and my experiences. I'll try to keep them somewhat brief...

PHASES OF MY RE-COVERY

PHASE I - Anorexia / Restrictive Eating

Growing up with kids and teenagers is tough shit these days. Well I guess it's always been that way if you really think about it. But especially nowadays with cell phones, tablets, social media, and the internet, easily accessible from our fingertips at any time. It's a whole different ball game when it comes to rumors being spread, pictures being sent and becoming viral, convenient and less confrontational cyber bullying, exposure to violence and dysfunction, and influences of unrealistic beauty standards for young kids to compare themselves to, to strive towards, and to and live up to.

I know far too many people that got bullied, and way worse than I ever did. But what I did get still struck right to my core and directly influenced my thought patterns, behaviors, and decisions growing up. I had friends tell me I was the fattest friend in 3rd grade when I wasn't even a chubby kid. I got made fun of for my blonde hairy arms and legs or my supposed mustache hair. I got teased for my awesome sense of style of grapefruit print capris and matching top with a rolling backpack. I got teased for my birthmarks and hairstyles. As I entered middle school and then high school after hitting puberty, I got teased for having an A-cup bra and "mosquito bite" boobs (which the insecurities of this, led me to getting a boob job at only 17 years old!) I got teased for my sweat patches under my arm pits. I got teased for my pimples on my face, chest, and back. I got teased for my chubby fingers. I got bullied for being a slut, a hoe, a bitch, or for being "easy" even though I was not. I got hate comments all over different social media platforms, and rumors or gossip being spread via text, word of mouth or social media as well. I lost dear friends and got kicked even when I was down with no one else around. I got taken advantage of and was belittled. I got called a ditz and dumb.

I'll leave it at that, but the sad truth is, this happens to a lot of kids in school growing up. They're all real, hurtful, and degrading. They pave a road for the development of dysfunction, insecurity, and emotional instability. They can create eating disorders in some or it can create violence, substance abuse, or any other harmful behavior in others.

My first eating disorder took place at a young age, starting around 14 years old. (No names will be named, as I am simply telling the story for this book's purpose to spread awareness, as I have moved on from this, and choose to not dwell on the past.) I had something traumatic happen with a guy, who was 18, and I was 14. Long story short, I said no no no, he was older, and bigger than me; I was shy, naive, and scared. He got me to do things I had never even heard of before, being only 14. This night is where a light appeared in front of us. I was ecstatic to get the F*@! out of this situation. It was the police as they had gotten a call from a neighborhood member. They took us to the police station because they saw what was going on, yet either he had a convincing story or they had a burn on for me/younger girls in our small town. I still do not know, but they treated me like crap, made me feel worthless, very condescending in a way that would make anyone question their own character, even when it's not the truth. The things they said dug deep into my core, and that night changed me from there on out.

Word spread around town and school quickly. I entered school with a whole reputation that didn't even resonate with me and was false. Nobody believed me, and how I didn't want it, not even my best friend. The cops didn't believe me and made me feel so horrible I can't even tell you how they treated me. Told me I was a liar, made me feel like a tramp, to say things lightly. My parents didn't believe me and seemed to take sides with the cops. (I can't blame them, grown adult cops are supposed to be the trustworthy ones, right?) The other hurtful thing was, my boyfriend, who I was head over heels for who I met shortly after this in the beginning of the school year, with his trust issues, didn't even believe me and gave me guff for it, making it seem like I wanted it, from the rumors he had heard.

I had everyone against me; no one believed me. That's how people get, and I understand now. The whole story got distorted and twisted. I tired of trying to explain and stick up for myself. Eventually, I went on believing I was the one at fault, it was all my fault, and the other guy got off scott-free, with no label, other than getting applauded for his hook up, while I, being a girl these days, got off with the title of a slut and a DG, "dirty girl."

I took on this story as my own, because if everyone else believed it, why shouldn't I? I shut down and cut off this memory not to have to re-live it or think about it. No matter how much I was asked to talk about it, by family, therapists, counselors, etc. I just suppressed it deeper. Little did I know it affected me subconsciously from there on out. But I had no desire to talk about it to anyone anymore, even thought my parents pushed it in therapy, and I thank them for caring so much.

Constantly being told something untrue about you, harsh rumors being spread, and even your most loved ones aren't on your side, you start to question yourself as a person, and you lose all self-esteem, and confidence in yourself. It's contagious, especially in the teenage years, when you are still in the stage of developing your "sense of self" and are not strong enough to stand in your "truth." If you don't even know what to stand for, how can you?

The other thing was, if people believe it, you get this almost anarchy type of feeling, where you say to yourself, well "screw it"; if everyone's going to believe it, then I might as well give them a show worth talking about. After that, the rest of my high school years were very dysfunctional. I definitely lost myself and was acting different than I ever had and almost constantly acted a certain way to fit the mold everyone had painted for me and win their approval.

I then took on the role of people pleasing and wanted to act in a way that would get people to like me. That's what this whole experience taught me: do what you're told to avoid conflict. (which is absurd, and you should never succumb to others' wishes against your own will and needs if you know and respect your self-worth.) This began my dance of pleasing, performing, perfecting, and proving.

I then I started sleeping around to get the external feelings of acceptance, and desire, and "love" (so I thought), since I couldn't get it elsewhere, and after the whole incident with the 18-year-old guy, it taught me how to act to get attention, whether in a good or bad way.

Since I lost all my good true friends I had from grade school I hung out with the wrong crowd and had to act a certain way. As you act like something long enough, you take on the part easily, and it comes more naturally. This is not a good thing, because every day I acted this part was another day I lost my true self even more. I took up drinking, drugs, and partying, because with this, I could numb how depressed I was feeling, hurt from all the drama going on with my boyfriend at the time (a toxic relationship), and with all the girls I had troubles with.

From then on, I continued with this unstable roller-coaster, on-and-off, emotionally-taxing relationship (you know those?). My boyfriend and I hurt each other; I was dealing with my issues, and he was with his childhood issues; it was unfortunate we caused each other to experience even more hurt we inflicted on each other (mentally and emotionally) than we were already dealing with.

This is where I first developed a strong eating disorder. I ate little and inconsistently, losing weight, quickly! Yet, as the weight came off, and fairly quickly I might add, I started to *love* the results. I was even told by a guy friend of mine how emaciated and scary I was looking, but instead of taking this criticism and changing it, I took it as a compliment and liked it, for some ridiculously odd reason!

I thought my ex might would finally want to be with me again (we were having major problems). He had deep seated issues he was dealing with prior, so I didn't realize he was too caught up in his own stuff; no matter what I did, it would not change his mind or the situation. So, I just kept with the eating disorder. It was the only thing I gained a sense of control over, and it seemed to get his attention.

Within that emotional rollercoaster of a relationship, he was always nitpicking and subtly pointing out my flaws. Although this could have been innocently, I still took it in a negative way, because I wasn't strong enough not to let it affect my confidence. He was picky with appearance and materialism, and projected his insecurities on me, which made me even more insecure than I already was. Even when it came to me tucking my shirt into my shorts or wearing different sunglasses, I would get some critical remark for my decisions. It made me obsessed with my external appearance and pleasing him, so to get his approval, I lost myself trying to love him and live up to his standards, rather than loving myself and defining my own standards for myself, by myself. Everything I did was for him, wondering if he would like it, or if it would get his attention, or if he would approve, or what would he do or say. This was not all his fault though; it was my insecurities and lack of self-love that drove my behaviors.

Since I couldn't control what was going on around me, the relationship with my boyfriend, the rumors, the drama, the hate, and the hurt, I found I could find control within restrictive eating habits; I found I could control my weight loss and food intake. It comforted me knowing I could at least control that.

I would not eat for days, or if I did, it would be something light earlier in the day, so I could get more drunk later that night. I became very moody, irritable, and depressed. If I were at a friend's house and I had the opportunity, I would have a massive binge, but then restrict afterwards to compensate for it.

My playful personality started to go out the loo; even one of my best friends made comments of this, saying I wasn't the same "Kayla" she loved to have fun with and have water balloon fights with, and be weird with. She said I was changing, and she didn't like it. Sadly, I didn't care. I was numb. I didn't want to continue playing school sports. I even lied about not making it on the volleyball team that year, so I wouldn't have to go anymore.

I didn't want to eat or drink water anymore, because when I ate or drank water in the morning, I would become bloated and I just wanted a flat tummy! I spent my lunch money on drugs rather than food and would do without food all day.

Thankfully, my parents were concerned with my behavior and drug/alcohol addictions, and I was sent to the Behavioral Medical Center (BMC), an outpatient rehabilitation center. I went in kicking and screaming, but had no choice but to attend. My therapist there was amazing, and I grew to enjoy going there. By the end of the few months attending, I can gladly say I was clean and sober and ready to move on from the lifestyle of drugs (but not yet the eating disorder, since still, nobody knew I had an eating disorder, to my knowledge). This was after something I read in one of the books at the BMC, which set off a lightbulb moment, but also after one night....

One night, I truly felt as if my world were ending, and that I would die from starvation combined with some cough medicine to get high. I felt as if nothing else mattered anymore as I faced the reality of my mortality. Fortunately, I survived, and after that, I was done with the drugs. And when I'm done and commit, I'm done, so yea I was done. I am good at doing things cold turkey. Although, I still smoked weed or had the occasional drink after this, like your "normal person" (whatever that is these days), all the binge drinking, hard core drugs, and pain killers, I was through with.

Fast forward to the age of 16-17. I graduated early after going on home study from all the drama and negativity going on at school. I then moved out to Santa Monica to go to College of Esthetician school. I took the drama, dysfunction, and eating disorder with me.

Even my roommates and fellow classmates in Santa Monica would comment on how skinny I was. But that just fueled the fire, and I wanted to keep going! Luckily, I had the Adderall (amphetamines) "for school" because it helped suppress my appetite, and I could go long without even getting hungry. This is where I started fainting and blacking out. This alarmed me to an extent, but I had more "important things to focus on" such as getting my ex back and taking cool pictures for social media. What a fulfilling life, eh?

PHASE II - Over exercising/Fitness Modeling/ Competing/Restrictive Dieting

At 18, I moved back home and continued at a local college. At first, I hated working out, but then it turned in to a full-blown addiction and obsession. I started to workout out with my mom going to yoga, personal training sessions, and even some boot camp classes. I would almost faint with these too, because I still was not eating, but trying to exert myself. I also got a job at my previous seasonal life-guarding job and even blacked out on the job there after drills one morning from not eating.

Mind you, I still was on and off with my ex-boyfriend, and since he was into bodybuilding and working out since a young age, (I'm talking bodybuilding competition at Venice Beach when he was 16 and placing) I connected the dots to me working out and impressing him. We ran into each other at this same local gym, so it was hard not to want to show off and impress him that I was now going to the gym too and working out more. He always wanted me to be the girlfriend to workout with him and be a fit couple at the gym, but I just never had the interest when we were younger. I also didn't want to get sweaty around him. HA, can you imagine?! So, all this working out, well you can guess, it eventually turned from being boring and suckish to becoming a challenge and an obsession.

I met a new guy soon after; he was a trainer at the gym and was older than me. Initially, it was to make my ex jealous, but it turned out to be a good trade-off relationship and friendship, starting from several dates, to soon a declared couple.

I learned a lot from him, gratefully so, since he was a personal trainer, and I worked out every day and sometimes twice a day, with a yoga class at my college near the gym. I loved working out, and I mean, I was obsessed, and it was turning into an *unhealthy* obsession. I could not miss a workout.

My boyfriend then felt as if our relationship had turned into just 'workout partners' rather than 'boyfriend and girlfriend' about 6 months in, which hurt him. It's sad to say, but I honestly didn't care in the moment; I was emotionally withdrawn from not eating, depleted from working out too much, and just too wrapped up in my own success with working out and making a name for myself, and becoming some "perfect healthy fit chick."

I researched more and more, becoming all-consumed. I tweaked my diet, and here's where things got messy. This is where I started the high-protein, low-carb, low-fat, "clean and lean" bodybuilding diet. I ate every 2-3 hours on the dot. I prepped my meals. I had chicken, tilapia, or egg whites at almost every meal, and steamed veggies. No oils, no salt, no fat, no sugar, so "clean and healthy" according to most, right?! NOT! This is where my health REALLY suffered.

The mindset of people pleasing had still been haunting me; I felt I needed to get attention, acceptance, and love from external sources, rather than from within, more than ever. I became well-known as a fitness chick on Instagram and Facebook with my followers climbing quickly over 20k+. I got several magazine features and had several sponsors. Things were looking good (from the outside), but on the inside, I was in a prison, a living hell. I cried in the mornings having to do the fasted cardio, and then again at night. I hated working out, as if it were my job. I hated every bite of meal prep I had to consume and gagged at times. I would project my miserable state on those around me by getting pissed if they were eating 'junk', because deep down, if I couldn't have it, nobody could. I became the 'food Nazi' of the house; I was miserable to live with, to be around, and I was miserable for myself.

Once I started booking photoshoots, I took everything to the next level with starvation, because what it takes to get photoshoot ready is insane. Cutting salt, even cutting egg whites because they had too much sodium. (comical, now) I was taking diuretics, only eating 'dry' raw oats, meat, and some steamed veggies. I was still working out as normal, even with absolutely no energy. I literally felt like a walking corpse for the week or two before the shoot (maybe the corpse of the corpse).

This would follow with a massive binge after the shoot. All I could think about during the shoots were what I would get to eat after and planning it all out as I went through the motions of the shoot. Same with the bikini competitions, not only me, but everyone backstage were like starving stray dogs, consumed with thoughts of food that couldn't wait to get the show over, so they could go pig out. That's all we talked about, what foods we liked, our favorite cheat meals, what we were eating to diet down for the competition, etc.

I wondered why I had lost my sex drive for the first time in my life (it was always strong) and why I became mega bloated and gassy and having massive digestion problems. I was bloated when I ate prior in the first phase, but this took bloating to a whole other level. It was constant and very uncomfortable. I lost my energy so drastically that I could barely walk up the 10 stairs to go to my college classes. I had to rely on pre-workouts and the Adderall AND a black coffee to get energy to go to the gym.

I dreamt and salivated about my "cheat meal" on the weekends, and all I could think about was what I'd have for the cheat meal (or what turned into a cheat *day*). After the cheat meal, I'd still be wanting more, even after being stuffed to the brim, feeling like I would pop. I'd dread going back to my diet the next day and couldn't wait until the next weekend for the cheat meal. I'd plan and write out exactly what I would eat days before. My life was all-consumed with food, but I would not let myself indulge unless it was a 'designated' cheat day. I could not care less to have relationships (besides my gym partners), go snowboarding (which I loved prior), or do any normal things in life. I was consumed in this lifestyle. I missed out on traveling opportunities because it would've been 'too hard' to travel with meal prep and eating every 2-3 hours and the daily training. I carried my "6-pack" lunch pail with me every time I left the house filled with my 5-6 nasty bland meals I'd have to choke down every couple hours.

There was one night, when I truly felt as if I were facing death again, and I begged for another day, and another chance, that I'd stop (which I didn't yet). My heart felt weak, but pounding, as if it would be its last beats. I cannot express how this feeling felt, but I know it was very frightening, and I'm very thankful I survived.

I lost myself even more within this phase and became more obsessed about my external appearance above all. And even then, I still wasn't satisfied nor happy with my body and felt I needed to keep losing fat and gaining muscle, even though I had absolutely no fat to lose. I still found other things I didn't like about my body to focus on, such as my scoliosis, or my "nonexistent" belly flap, or my pimples, or my skin tone; I mean anything and everything!

I would constantly pinch my absent 'belly fat', flapping the absent 'fat' on my arms and legs, constantly looking in the mirror, flexing my arms and abs, lifting my shirt to see what my stomach looked like, and I mean constantly; that was the first thing I did waking in the morning. I liked my stomach in the morning, because you're dehydrated and not digesting foods from sleeping for hours, so I'd take my Instagram photos then. Little did all my followers know that is NOT what I looked like walking around all day (nor the other fitness accounts they were also following). I was bloated to the brim, not as tight and dry from drinking water and eating food the rest of the day. I'd find the best lighting and pose a certain way to manipulate the way I looked. It's all so fake it's humorous now.

PHASE III - Bulimia, Binge/Purge

Okay, so how could this all *not* lead into a full-on binge (and purge in my case) stage?! It's the inevitable result from all the restriction and starvation (yep, even with the excuse I was eating my 5-6 meals a day that I liked to justify with). It lasted daily for about 9 months. And I never told a soul, even my boyfriend. I only told my diary.

After the last competition and the gorging session afterward, I just quit on everyone. I was done with it all. Mentally and physically, I had had it. I stopped posting on my Instagram and Facebook account, I cut out all contact with my coach, my workout partner, and with all the photographers I had plans with. I had enough. I could no longer do it anymore. I was suffering too much and too unhappy to continue that lifestyle. Plus, I was extremely grossed out by all the chicken and tilapia I had to eat 4-5 times a day. I definitely went vegetarian for a while after, as a result from the bodybuilding diet.

I was so confused as to what was happening. I honestly thought I was just losing my willpower after all these years. I felt I was losing my control I had maintained all these years. I felt weak and disappointed in myself; I felt disgusted and ashamed. I felt like a glutton and greedy. I felt I had failed myself, the people following me, my clients, and my family.

I did not know binging and purging was a side effect from the restrictive dieting I had been on. So, without the awareness and still in denial, trying to continue with my restrictive dieting, I still tried to fight the binging. I'd go a couple days, maybe a week if I was lucky, being diligent on my diet, but low and behold, I'd binge. I'd go through jars of nut butters, gallons of ice cream, all-you-can-eat-sushi, and boxes of granola/protein bars. I could never satisfy my hunger, no matter how much I was in pain from the fullness.

By this time, my hair started falling out, I became dizzy at my job, walking to school, or even sitting in class. I'd have bouts of vertigo where I felt I would fall over or that my equilibrium was way off. I was still bloated as heck, worse by this point, and it was a constant 8-month pregnant looking bloat. I also was starting to develop multiple food allergies as time went on. I even got an *award* from my job at the time for *"Being the Most Allergic to Everything."* This is not a joke, I truly got a printed and sealed award for that. What a joke! (I still adore the people at that job and can laugh at the humor behind it.)

My sex drive was still absent, and I'd always be making excuses why I couldn't have sex or be intimate with my boyfriend. I wasn't even 'there,' as a girlfriend, or a friend, because I had no brain space or motivation to be present, give and receive love, have fun, or live a normal life. I had no energy. I was depending on shots of espresso daily to keep me going. I was very emotional still and just wanted to feel better.

I found black mold in my closet several months into this, and I made that my reason to blame all my symptoms on, so I could stay in denial of my problem and not face the reality of it all. I could not see the restricting, over exercising, binging and purging was the main root of it all! This just took away the responsibility that needed to be taken on my part that I had a problem, and that I needed to change.

On that New Year's Eve, I made a promise to myself to stop purging, and I did it! I was eating tons and not allowing myself to purge it up. I still could not focus in school or function as a human in life. I was definitely unhappy and only existing, not living. My health was only getting worse each day.

PHASE IV - Orthorexia

Within the beginning of the year, after New Year's, I tried Paleo, GAPS, FOODmaps, and protocols like these to heal my gut and all the negative health symptoms I was facing. None of it worked, so I went vegan.

I was only vegan for about 5 months before I found raw veganism and then fruitarianism. I bounced back between the two versions of raw veganism, over the next few years, and then a year of cooked vegan. Raw veganism had claims for promising results that could "heal me" for good, I thought. I can say though, this phase took away every aspect of my health and amplified what I was already experiencing and was, by far, the worst point I had been in.

My intentions were simply to heal myself from all these negative symptoms I was facing by this time, from all the

previous damage from restrictive dieting for the past almost decade. I got into detoxing, cleansing, fasting, juice
fasting, intermittent fasting, you name it. I spent hundreds
on supplements, probiotics, enzymes, organ cleanses
(herbal), vitamins, coaching sessions, etc. I was in it to
heal myself, once and for all. I thought I would be the
healthiest human because I was on "the most optimal and
pure diet that humans were biologically designed for!" I
became obsessed and was just as restrictive, just in a whole
new way. I was so sold on this way of living, even though I
still was feeling horrible, and my health was getting worse
by the day; I still preached this way of living as if it were
the golden ticket, the holy grail, the answers to everyone's
problems! Well, I was annoying, that's what I was. I was in
denial and brainwashed. I became "vegan-gelical," preaching to the world that everyone needed to become vegan,
and if you weren't vegan, you were ignorant, and evil, and
a murderer, and destroying the planet, as if veganism was
the *only* answer to saving the planet and animals' from
monstrous living conditions. My intentions were good, but
I couldn't see this diet was destroying my health, even
more so than the previous restrictive diets!

At first, I experienced heightened energy and clearer skin.
But that was short-lived. One day, after just finishing a
hike and driving down the boulevard, suddenly, it hit me
like a literal tornado in my head, and that moment, I had
the worst case of brain fog ever; that was where it started.
The brain fog never went away for the next several years,
and it was one of my worst complaints. It felt as if I never
could clearly think or process thoughts anymore, and any-
where I walked, I felt as if I would fall over. 24/7, I was in a
constant state of fog.

This made me want to "cleanse, heal, and detox" even
more to heal myself from the brain fog and all the other
symptoms I faced. I started not to be able to tolerate any

cooked foods; even steamed peeled zucchini and boiled artichoke made me ill.

At first, I was not calorie restricting. I was on the diet where you are not restricting calories, but eating well over 2,000 calories a day, and more often at 3,000+ calories, "smashing in the carbs" from just fruit and raw vegetables. Even with this, I kept dropping weight, and I did not need to lose any weight, but needed weight GAIN. The point being, I experienced different phases of orthorexia, depending on the diet, guru, or doctor, and not all of them were restrictive in calories, but in food groups.

Each phase, I became weaker and worse, and the symptoms became more pronounced. I thought it was because the cooked food was toxic and poison to my body (as I was told to believe by the raw food community and leaders), and I had to limit or avoid it, which almost forced me to continue being raw.

I eventually went on juice cleanses, and in this phase, I got down to 90 lbs. (I'm 5'6"), and I looked emaciated, something I never looked like even in my anorexia days; although I was super skinny, I was not under 100 lbs. maybe 110-115 lbs. I could not put weight back on, no matter what different raw diet I tried (raw ketogenic, raw high fruit, even Body Ecology). Hmmm I wonder why?!

Again, I felt I would truly die, but this time, it was every night for months and years, and I either begged for another chance or didn't even care if I passed because of how bad I was suffering, and how I felt there was no way out. I had many bouts of crying spells, many thoughts of suicide and driving my car off the road, and even thoughts to head to Oregon for Euthanasia.

I tried to contact the raw food community, and every time I expressed what was happening and what I was experiencing, it was always downplayed and turned around as if I was doing something wrong. Yet, I was doing everything right, according to the guidelines and rules of every healing approach I tried. This couldn't be the case! But I listened and just kept pushing and "digging deeper."

At this point, my brainwashed mind left me with no other alternatives, but this path to "true optimal health" and any other way was bad and "wrong" and I'd end up with many diseases and maladies if I ate any other way. The irony was, I felt I was *developing* many diseases on this "ideal" raw vegan diet, yet I still thought the other routes and diets were the causative ones, and I was only experiencing "healing crisis." Healing crisis, if true, should definitely not last for the years they did for me.

I was severely constipated, even on high water rich and fiber rich foods (I had to do daily, sometimes multiple per day, enemas for over a year). All my foods were coming out undigested (literally came out looking the way they went in), I would get so winded after eating, even just a "mono meal" of fruit, I'd have to lie down and take several naps a day (for these few years, it didn't go away). My bones creaked more as I moved around and walked, my hair was so thin even the tiniest of hair ties would barely do (and I'd always had thick hair!). My belly was more bloated than ever, my heart was always beating irregularly, and felt like bradycardia. I was having so much trouble digesting any morsel of food. I was so cold, it was unbearable even with 4 layers of clothes, sitting by the fire, and the heater blasting. I couldn't have thoughts other than food or nutrition related ones. I couldn't even walk around my block, because I was so weak. I was so emaciated everyone was worried, including myself. I wanted to gain weight so badly, and would stuff myself with raw foods to gain weight, but I remained gaunt.

After the first year and a half of being strictly fruitarian and juice fasting, I tried other restrictive "healing protocols." I tried everything, and believe it when I say it, I stuck to the exacts with each set of rules. I tried intermittent fasting (all versions), low-oxalate diet, low-fructan diet, high carb low fat (both raw and cooked versions), high protein/low carb/ low fat (bodybuilding style), ketogenic (both vegan and animal product versions, raw and cooked), Body Ecology, 80/10/10, McDougall, Nutritarian (Dr. Fuhrman), sproutarian (Hippocrates Institute), Natural Hygiene (Dr Herbert Shelton), extended water fasting, Master Fast, green juice fasting, fruit juice fasting, ("liquidarian"), mono-fruit fasting, fat fasting, oil fasting, white rice/fruit diet (Dr Walter Kempner), nightshade free, raw vegan, regular vegan, fruit-free, grain-free, starch-free, oil-free, salt-free, sugar-free, caffeine-free, phytate-free, vinegar-free, low-histamine diet, elimination diets of all sorts, coffee and other kinds of enemas, liver/gallbladder flushes, and honestly, there were more. I just don't want to list everything.

I tried McDougals Starch Solution approach to the vegan diet being high starch. I felt disgusting being as bloated as I was. I was binging on sweet potatoes, oatmeal and white/ brown rice. I was still not improving, except I got some energy back.

No amount of foods could satisfy me. Even if I stuffed myself with 20 bananas or a couple pounds of potatoes in a meal and felt physically stuffed to the brim, I still was hungry for something mentally; my body was still searching for other nutrients I wasn't giving it. I felt, if I kept with raw long enough or cooked vegan long enough, my cravings would totally disappear and my taste buds would change. I thought all my symptoms were going to magically heal, at some point, if I kept persisting with this diet, when obviously, it was not working for me.

So, after several months of binging on cooked starches, I decided I needed to go on a water fast (oh lordie) to heal all my physical ailments once and for all! I went to stay at a supervised clinic in Northern California, one of the most trusted clinics with some of the top doctors in the field! It didn't help me. I only craved food more than ever during and after that fast. My hunger did not subside after the first few days as promised. I felt like I was dying during the fast, so I had to end it sooner than planned. After the water fast, I went back to raw vegan and intermittent fasting. I continued to feel ill, so I felt, well if I'm going to suffer, I might as well suffer in paradise, right? So, I moved to Hawaii spontaneously, as I'd been wanting to move there for years. I thought, finally, I'd be in raw fruit heaven and no one would bug me about my eating disorder and need to gain weight and eat! I'd have an abundance of high nutrient tropical fruit to feast on!

Little did I know, Hawaii would give me the chance to change and wake up to my problem. After being in Hawaii, within a couple weeks, I could begin recovery. How?! To say it simply, I had the help of two friends who opened my eyes, providing support and wisdom, as to what I needed to change.

Living in Hawaii on an organic farm, then in a van, and then under the roof of one of my friends, vulnerable, dependent on others for transportation and grocery shopping; I couldn't prepare foods as I wanted... *This took away my control of food*; I took what I could get. My friend at the time was encouraging me to heal, as he had gone through similar experiences in his past. So, I had his support and insight to help me see I needed to change, and not to fear foods, to stop cutting out foods, and instead to add back in everything. Eating normal meals, more than just fruit and veggies, gave me just the nourishment I needed to think clearly, awaken my appetite, and show my body it wasn't in a famine anymore....

I followed my intuition and cravings and what my body was asking for, despite the ill feelings, and helped it out by RESTING and allowing the process to just be, and lo and behold, I got out and got my life back after some time... it was simply because I was weak; every organ was weak, and the energy of the foods coming in were helping to wake up the body and nourish and strengthen every cell.

No matter how hard I tried to go back to my old thought patterns, it was already broken as if the beast had finally been released; there was no turning back. For several months, I still tried to fight it...I thought I had lost my "self-control" again that I "re-mastered" during my or-thorexic days. I felt I had become weak, and the "addic-tion" was controlling me... the "addiction" of cooked, fatty, and animal product foods... (all these dogmas and my mind had me thinking all these thoughts from the raw food/vegan world!!). I felt so guilty and ashamed! I still fought for months trying to hold onto the restrictions of certain foods and food groups; I still wanted to eat as "clean" as possible. But over time, as I kept feeding my body, it was clearer to me what truly was giving me health and healing and giving me my life back. I could rewire my thoughts not to try to strive after raw-veganism or regular veganism at all anymore and be *okay* with it.

But what I started to realize was...it wasn't an "addiction." I wasn't addicted to these foods! It was the fuel my body so desperately needed and had been craving for YEARS. As I continued feeding my body regular foods (and having many *necessary* binges) ... the better I felt. Slowly, I cared more about how *good* I was feeling, more than the weight I was gaining (part of recovery obviously). I did not allow myself to purge the binges, even though those thoughts aroused again.

I felt more energized, my digestion was healing. My period, sex drive, laughter, joy, and strength was returning!! I truly felt I had gotten my life back. I went out with loved ones without having to think about what I'd do about food; the relief and freedom this gave me is priceless. The day I realized I had a problem was the day I never looked back...and I got my health and life back! The rest is history, and I'm grateful for every moment of it!

Conclusion of My ED Journey
You know what worked and what I'm still on? The Kayla Rose Kotecki diet. And I suggest you go on the " *'insert your name here'* Diet." The guidelines and rules are to listen to your body, your appetite, and your cravings and not compare to anyone else and what they're doing, preaching, or saying.

There is a lot of noise, a lot of confusion, and a lot of misunderstandings around the recovery process for eating disorders; I want to explain what is expected and what to do to have full and permanent recovery. The catch is, you must commit 100%, and I'll keep reminding you of that, because without your commitment, recovery cannot happen. Everything you need to know about recovery is in this book, as I spent every waking hour researching and experimenting different recovery methods. Don't go through *all* the relapses and trial and errors I had to, because I've now written in this book what is to be expected and how to recover permanently.

"In the 2006 study, disordered eating behaviors for weight control, such as fasting, laxative abuse, smoking,

vomiting, chewing food but not swallowing and slimming pills were dangerously present and frequent in girls as young as 12 years old. There appears to be a sharp increase in these dangerous behaviors after pubertal development, which has been suggested by previous authors. Among older girls, these unhealthy behaviors were more common, with as many as one fifth of 16– 19-year-old girls regularly fasting for two days or more to try to control their weight." (National Youth Cultures of Eating Study)

Make recovery a priority and your number one focus in life right now. You have the rest of your life to live, eat, have fun, exercise moderately, and work, but to do so, you need to heal and be healthy, which requires you to go through the recovery process. It's often too easy for people with busy jobs or school to "forget" to eat, take their break, or stay busy to avoid eating, but this behavior must stop. You must put your recovery as a priority. The quicker you restore your weight and eat over 3,500+ calories a day, the quicker your recovery will go and last. The more you relapse and avoid it, the longer you draw out the process. If you have to, put everything on hold in your life while you commit and go for it 100%.

STARVATION CON-SEQUENCES

REMEMBER, I was still alone throughout my recovery and did not have guidance. I was simply going off my intuition after I got the initial brain power to think straight for the first time after eating against my will at an encouraging and supportive friend's house.

*For the anorexic, or severely malnourished disordered eater, gaining weight is the prerequisite for mental recovery; you can't make an anorexic want to put on weight until he/she has gone ahead to do so already. "The mind may make the body sick, but only the body can help the mind be well again." (*PsychologyToday.com*)*

"More on The Great Starvation Experiment: The experiment was designed to increase understanding of human starvation. During the 6-month semi-starvation period, subjects (young, healthy men, both in robust physical and mental health) For the next twelve weeks (the control period of the experiment), Keys allowed them 3200 calories a day. He directed the men to maintain an active lifestyle, working jobs in the lab and walking a minimum of twenty-two miles a week.

When the first twelve-week period came to a close, the men were reduced to about 1560 calories a day and physical activities were also strictly controlled; the men experienced severe psychological problems such as Hysteria and Depression, hypochondria, preoccupation with food, reduction in sexual interest, social withdrawal, irritability/anger, vicarious pleasure in watching others eat, hoarding food, edema in extremities, amongst other things. As starvation progressed, toying with their food also increased. They smuggled bits of food and consumed them on their bunks in a long drawn out ritual. Cookbooks, menus, and information bulletins on food production became intensely interesting to many of the men who previously had little to no interest in the dietetics or agriculture. Meal times became the high point of their day. They grew irritable if they weren't served their food exactly on time, or if they had to wait too long in line. Although the food was quite bland, to the men it tasted delicious. Their heart rates fell significantly – from fifty-five beats per minute to thirty-five. This was their metabolism slowing down, and it was a sign that their bodies were trying to conserve calories.

They also reported not having regular bowel movements – only one per week. Their blood volume dropped ten percent, and their hearts shrank in size. The men developed edema (water retention). Their ankles, knees, and faces swelled – an odd physical symptom considering their otherwise skeletal appearance. There was also a decrease in basal metabolic rate (BMR) by 40% below normal. Dizziness, muscle soreness, reduced coordination, and ringing in the ears were also other side effects. They developed a whitening of their eyeballs as the blood vessels in their eyes shrank. The skin of some of the men developed a coarse, rough appearance as a result of the hardening of their hair follicles. The lack of body fat made it difficult for them to sit down for long periods of time because their bones would grind against the seats. They lingered over the food, savoring every bite. Often they "souped" their meals – mixing everything with water to make it seem as if there was more. Some participants avoided eating because they were fearful of weight gain, and did not see themselves as being too skinny, but instead thought everyone else was just fat compared to them.

Twenty-four-year-old Franklin Watkins began having vivid disturbing dreams of cannibalism in which he was eating the flesh of an old man. Then he grew angry and threatened to kill Keys and take his own life. Keys immediately dismissed Watkins from the experiment and sent him to the psychiatric ward of the university hospital. There, after a few days on a normal diet, Watkins appeared entirely normal again, so the hospital released him. Watkins' breakdown occurred just a few weeks into the starvation phase of the experiment.

Subject No. 20 stuffs himself until he is bursting at the seams, to the point of being sick, and still feels hungry; No. 120 reported that he had to discipline himself to keep from eating so much as to become ill; No. 1 ate until he was uncomfortably full; and subject No. 30 had so little control over the mechanics of "piling it in" that he simply had to stay away from food because he could not find a point of satiation even when he was "full to the gills." "I ate practically all weekend," reported subject No. 26, "and would just as soon have eaten six meals instead of three. Another man began to dig in garbage bins for food, and developed an enormous amount of eating followed by induced vomiting.

The last meal of the study was served on October 20, 1945. The men were subsequently free to depart and eat as they pleased. However, Keys convinced twelve of them to stay on at the lab for another eight weeks so he could monitor them during an "unrestricted rehabilitation" phase. Left to their own devices, Keys observed these men consume over 5000 calories a day, on average. And on occasion, some of them feasted on as many as 11,500 calories in a single day. For many months, the men reported having a sensation of hunger they couldn't satisfy, no matter how much they ate.

During the 3-month re-feeding stage of the experiment, many of the men lost control of their appetites and ate "more or less continuously. Those who lost control felt self-deprecated, disgusted, and self-critical for doing so. Keys concluded that in order to recover from starvation (1570 calories a day), and rebuild strength a person needs around 4000 calories a day. The group of volunteers who received a relatively small increment in calories during rehabilitation (400 calories more than during semi-starvation) had no rise in BMR for the first three weeks.

After about 8 months of referring their metabolism began to rise, most men reported their eating habits had normalized, although binge-eating continued to be a problem for several. They did not eat until they were obese, they in general, regained their original weight plus about 10% in the rehabilitation phase, and then their weight gradually declined towards the pre-experiment levels. The subjects who gained the most weight became concerned about their increased sluggishness, general flabbiness, and the tendency of fat to accumulate in their abdomen and buttocks. They had fears of weight gain, they often reported "feeling fat" and worried about acquiring distended stomachs.

The conclusion: These very healthy young men, within only a few months of a calorie-restricted diet, were in physical and psychological terms, suffering from various extreme forms of the symptoms associated with anorexia nervosa Keys highlighted the degree to which the amount we eat can alter both the mind and the body. Evolution apparently fashioned the human body to withstand long periods without food, and therefore if you give a substantial amount of recovery time after for the body to heal, starvation didn't appear to have any significant, long-term negative impacts on health."

In this study, the men were only in semi-starvation, not even full starvation, at 1,560 calories, yet what's often recommended to us by the *National Institute for Health* for dieting today is what those men were eating, at 1,200-1,500 calories a day, and even less than that! It's very common in this dieting age we live in today to be told and to feel comfortable to lose weight at only 1,570 calories a day. To most, this is even considered a healthy number to lose weight or even live on daily. Some may think this is too many calories to sustain, let alone consider it "starvation." Even the *US National Institute of Health* recommends us to eat 1,000 to 1,500 calories to lose weight these days! No wonder eating disorders are at an all-time high!

The men went 'mental' from physical starvation, even though they were perfectly fine prior to the study, with no signs of mental disease, having a normal relationship with food, normal mental and physical health, and normal non-obsessive behaviors. They went into the study with good intentions and committed to the cause to help the world better understand the effects of starvation around the globe.

Too often these days, people are facing horrible debilitating physical ailments from restrictive dieting, such as digestion problems, anxiety, paranoia, hormonal imbalance, obsessiveness, compulsiveness, loss of menses, loss of libido, fatigue, insomnia, and other signs of mental illness. Doctors that are unaware these people are suffering from restrictive disordered dieting and 'cannot find anything wrong with them physically through tests' assume they have a mental illness and are just making up the physical symptoms in their head and send them to a psychiatrist. This happened to me; in fact, after being such a happy little kid, known to "smile too much" things changed; throughout my teenage years, after my fitness competing and modeling days, later in my orthorexia stages of my ED, the doctors thought all the symptoms I was expressing were in my head because they couldn't diagnose me with anything from the results from their tests. They wanted to put me on psychiatric medications, because little did they know, I was suffering from restrictive dieting and malnutrition all that time, just in different ways throughout the years.

I was put on many concoctions with several drugs for depression, anxiety, ADD, mood instability, insomnia, birth control (to help PMS, depression, and acne), and more. Later, they wanted to put me on a bipolar medication, and that is when I was done with the prescription drugs, as they were not helping me and things were only getting worse. Fast forward to my recovery, I saw an improvement in my mood tremendously. My mom even noticed I no longer seemed to have the anger and temper to the extent I did (which was horrendously bad) when I was PMS'ing around my menstrual cycle (when it finally returned). I noticed this and noticed the signs of severe anxiety, depressiveness, and hopelessness lift.

It's not to say prescription drugs are never needed, but often, regarding restrictive eating disorders, the mental symptoms can often be mistaken as mental illness, rather than as a result from dieting, semi-starvation, and malnourishment. Nor is this not to say mental illness can often be what was already in place and was the contributing factor to the eating disorder to develop. For a lot of people, they are already depressed and mentally unstable before the eating disorder developed and actually developed the ED as a way to cope with their feeling of lack of control over their emotions.

One-third of all people who diet will end up on the eating disorder spectrum. While not all of them develop clinical cases, if left untreated they will experience lifelong anxieties and compulsions around food and weight gain. The condition can develop into a clinical case at any point due to life stressors (anything from a cold to a break-up). Over time, those with the condition will often slide up and down the spectrum, or express multiple facets of the spectrum at once (anorexia, restrict/reactive eating cycles, bulimia, orthorexia [extreme focus on healthy foods], and anorexia athletica [over-exercise]). Between the ages of 15 and 24, eating disorders are 12 times more deadly than all other leading causes of death combined for that age group, including car accidents. Death from those with an eating disorder can range from heart failure, to suicide. (EDInstitue.org)

As my weight came closer to "normal" again in recovery, the obsessiveness, the inflexibility of thought, socially withdrawn, feeling the need for a routine, the constant feeling of being cold, the lack of concentration, the insomnia, the hair loss, and dull skin, the physical effects of starvation and all else, diminished as predicted; the only way to overcome this was by regaining my weight. From a size 0 or even 00 in my orthorexia stage and a size 1 or 3 in my first couple stages, I got to a size 8/10 with a lot of muscle (not hard and defined), and by then, I didn't even care anymore about the weight gain, because I felt better, mentally and physically, than I ever did at my lower weights in my restrictive eating disorder days.

My experience gaining weight was humbling, because I was so judgmental towards everyone else around me who weighed more than 'average' (in my mind) and had very little empathy or understanding towards others who could not "lose the weight" despite everything they were trying. Not only did I have body dysmorphia for myself, but I had it for everyone around me. I got a taste of what it feels like to be at a higher weight, despite doing everything right and the frustration that comes with it, but also the judgments and pressures that society puts on us to be a certain way, and if we aren't just that, we are to feel disappointed, less than, and ashamed.

I appreciate and have a deep understanding of how strong and how much character these confident people in the world have and how much self-love they truly have for themselves, despite how the "numbers" and society defined them. It gave me a dose of humble tea. I wasn't so judgmental of everyone else and gave people a break for once, but I also had to learn how to give myself a break and find my self-value outside of my weight or appearance only. I got to learn how not to care what people think, because no matter how much I said in the past, about how much I didn't care what people thought, I was lying through my teeth, because that's all I thought about. As I realized all this and developed my own self-acceptance and appreciation, whatever I did, if I wore makeup, wore certain clothes, or how I acted, it was for me, because it was fun and it made *me* feel good, and was for no one other than myself from then on.

Your true personality and character is suppressed when starved, although when suffering from anorexia, you'll be convinced what you feel and present as your personality is just a mask, and until you gain weight, your personality cannot reemerge and come to light. My personality did within recovery; I felt just as playful as I did prior to starting my disordered eating ways since the age of 14. I also noticed my memories were coming back and was better able to think of good memories from childhood. I felt reconnected with my inner child, and it was liberating! When starved, your character and thoughts are dominated by malnourishment.

61

Some of the general symptoms relating to starvation and malnourishment from restriction are as follows:

-Amenorrhea; No menstruation or irregular menstruation
-Unhealthy, Brittle looking skin, hair, and/or nails; loss of hair more than usual
-Lack of Mental Concentration; brain fog
-Dizziness and/or Fainting; Seizure
-Obsession with food and anxiety around foods; Preoccupation with food
-Denial of hunger; Lying about how much food has been eaten
-Depression, anxiety, panic attacks, and nervousness
-Immune Deficiency; Constant illness due to a weakened immune system
-Mood swings, irritability, crying spells, easily annoyed
-Social Withdrawal; Lack of Emotion; Thoughts of Suicide
-Weight Loss; extreme
-Gaining weight easily, even when eating until fullness – gaining weight by eating 2000 calories or less a day
-Tired, fatigued, and weak
-Irregular Heart Rhythms; Low Blood Pressure
-Osteoporosis; loss of bone calcium, which may result in broken bones
-Sleep problems; insomnia
-Decreased Sex Drive
-Elevated Liver Enzymes
-Dehydration; feeling of dry fuzzy mouth or cotton mouth
-Lowered Body Temperature; Feeling cold all the time; cold feet and hands
-Digestive problems, such as constipation or diarrhea, nausea, stomachache
-Food intolerance; lowered capability to digest certain foods; extreme sensitivity to
foods you once where able to eat with no problem
-Nausea after eating

-Bloating and stomach distention, especially after meals
-Swelling from fluid under the skin / Water retention/
Edema: swollen stomach, ankles, face, puffy eyes
-Muscle, joint, or skin aches and pains; inflammation after
eating certain restricted foods
-Binge eating and messed-up hunger/ fullness signals
-Severely restricting food intake through dieting or fasting;
can include excessive exercise

*"Your starved state is making it impossible for you to
think flexibly enough to fully comprehend the possibility
of eating or living differently, or even the possibility of
wanting to think about and enjoy other things other than
food; it has been hidden from you who you really are, and
made you believe you are nothing but the anorexia or "the
state of trying to heal your body through caloric restricting and fasting." It is making the smallest piece of food
feel like too much or too "poisonous"; these reasons will be
why you will never have the desire to want to recover in
this starved state."*

I had to be sent to Hawaii, out of control, no car, no money, no freedom to do my own shopping, to force me to eat
the food my friend who took me in gave me to eat, and the
encouragement from him not to be fearful. It took those
first bowls of pasta with parmesan cheese, and then the
peanut butter binge the next day to initiate it. Sometimes,
you just have to take the leap of faith... dive in and take the
plunge full force... I was forced into it, and I'm thankful
that I was, but at the time, it made me very uncomfortable
and angry. His suggestions to try some bread and fish ag-
gravated me.

*"You have to seize all your feelings of despair, despera-
tion, hope, recklessness, and curiosity in order to make
yourself plunge into the first day and first meal of recovery. As long as you keep yourself going, keep eating,*

63

through the first difficult weeks, it will get easier and easier."

"Recovery from anorexia and disordered restrictive eating is not easy, but it is simple." All you must do is keep eating and raise your BMI above 19, ideally 20-25, and maintain your weight. Also, increase your weight even slightly above this healthy range or clinically determined as the "healthy range" for some time as you recover to achieve full recovery. This overshoot in weight can be a life saver and determinate in your success. It will all balance out with time, and I'll get more into that later.

One mouthful at a time, you can "live" again, rather than just "exist." You'll even get to a point where you won't want to go back and not care about the number of your BMI, because of how much better you *feel*, making recovery much easier to maintain. I love having my joy, energy, and strength back! You will too!

If I would have known what to do better, I would have started earlier and not had so many relapses along the way (no regrets though, of course. I learned what I needed in the way I had to). But I did SO often feel mentally guilty and ashamed and disgusted that I still tried to go back and hold onto every bit of raw veganism/cooked veganism. I'd last only a day, or maybe up to 3, and a couple times up to 7 days. This went on for months even after I moved back to California to continue my recovery process. Because every time I went back to restricting food groups, no matter how many raw food calories were consumed, it never satisfied my body's needs like the cooked starches, and saturated animal fats and proteins. I'd end up binging at night, because I wasn't getting what I needed during the day from the raw vegan diet. Even the cooked vegan diet did not satisfy me; it wasn't until I added the eggs, butter, some meat, and dairy products and then I truly saw breakthroughs. All this relapsing and yo- yo-ing delayed my recovery by months.

Many people experience this yo-yoing through the beginning or even first 8 months of recovery (as I did), still holding onto the fear and not fully embracing or trusting the process. Every time they retain water or gain weight, they go back to restricting. They think recovery isn't working for them; they panic and fall back into restriction because they are experiencing *normal* recovery symptoms. Your body just becomes so confused with this going back-and-forth, and this does not give it a sense of ease or feeling it's safe and okay to come out of starvation mode.

Let's talk about the popular myth about an 'increased life-span from caloric restriction.' Matt Stone explains it well in the end of his free book, <u>Diet Recovery</u>, and the beginning of his small priced book, <u>Diet Recovery 2</u>...

"An increasingly popular myth is the idea that it's good to have a low metabolism —and that if we burn energy more slowly we will live longer. Much of this stems from laboratory research showing that severe calorie restriction (like eating half of what you normally eat) prolongs life in several species like fruit flies, rats, monkeys... But, like most research, this prolongation of life is taken completely out of context and then turned around and applied to adult humans living and interacting in the real world. It ignores aspects of drastic and game-changing significance like...

1) The only people successful at permanently reducing calorie intake by at least half are those that develop an eating disorder, the deadliest known psychological disease, which affects 11 million Americans, mostly young women. Statistics I've seen suggest a 25-year reduction of life expectancy once you've been diagnosed with an eating disorder (and dieting/intentional calorie restriction at a young age is the top "risk factor" for developing one).

2) Humans are surrounded by endless abundance and temptation for food, and with real people in the real world, cutting calories by half leads to massive rebound hyperphagia (pigging out —as is seen in yo-yo dieting and every human calorie-restriction trial ever conducted).

3) Calorie restriction experiments are done with animals from birth, which allows their bodies to develop to be smaller in size. When comparing members of the same species, the smaller members usually have a much higher life expectancy than larger members (for example, small dogs live much longer than big dogs, despite radically higher mass-specific metabolic rates). This is a hugely significant difference, and the bodies of the creatures can develop at a rate that makes the low-calorie intake suffi-cient —but this calorie intake is insufficient and causes rapid degeneration when the calorie level is cut after adulthood has already been reached. Comparing calorie restriction from birth to calorie restriction begun in adulthood is a completely invalid comparison.

4) Calorie-restricted laboratory animals display many characteristics of neurosis, anxiety, and social/behavioral disorders. Thinking that cutting calories will lead to a long and prosperous life in a human is a total fantasy that ignores what science has already shown us.

5) It may not be the reduction in calories that causes a prolongation of life. Some studies on the restriction polyunsaturated fats (which oxidize and cause aging the fastest), or restricting certain amino acids (like trypto-phan or methionine), yield the same life extension without the restriction of total food intake.

6) A laboratory is a sterile environment, and even if the calorie restricted animals lived longer and did have a verifiably slower metabolic rate (pound for pound I don't think they do), it's hard to compare this to the real world. The real world is filled with opportunistic organisms and other pathogens, and a high metabolism controls the strength of the immune system completely. A high body temperature –a result of a high metabolism, protects from invasion just like a fever wipes an infection out. More importantly, it is obvious when looking at the real world what happens when food becomes scarce –famines lead to widespread disease and infection at astronomically higher rates.

In fact, even a simple drop in body fat levels due to inadequate calorie intake lowers the hormone leptin –the master hormone well-understood to regulate appetite, metabolism, and immune system potency. It also raises the stress hormone cortisol, the primary aging and immunosuppressive hormone. Of course, you're now thinking "Outgrow our food supply? Humans clearly haven't done that!" And you're right. Food is more abundant than ever, and your typical person is looking to lose fat not gain it. We'll get to that in a minute (you can read more in his book <u>here</u>) *but let's say for now that you can have a low metabolism because of a shortage of anything, from lack of sleep to lack of certain nutrients –not just overall calories. And on any given day in the United States for example, 45% of the population reports actively being on some kind of diet –which often triggers the same famine physiology as a real famine."*

If you're one to think lifespan is only extended from calorie restriction or a perfectly clean diet... think again. Health goes so much further than diet and what we put in our mouths. Quality of life, happiness, sex drive, digestion, and other important functions far overshadow the importance of lifespan that are also not considered. The longest living elderly folks I've met, I tried to squeeze out their secrets, hoping I'd hear they were on the most perfect diet, and that's why they lived so long and are in good health and good spirits... but I was disappointed each time, because rather than that, they told me they eat whatever they want and never restricted, and they drank their glass of alcohol (not excessively), but their real secrets were, they are surrounded by a community of loving and supportive souls, they laugh a lot, they don't stress so much about stupid things in life, they dance, rest, are playful, and are just more optimistic people.

Anyway, onward bound: Let's look at the goals you want to accomplish soon...

MENTAL ASPECTS

CHANGE YOUR DAMN STORY! Please, change it. Change the story you tell yourself about how you react to foods, how you feel about foods, or just your story about your relationship with food and body. Change your story of old learned and conditioned belief systems and ego driven behaviors. Instead of saying "Oh, I react negatively to these certain foods," change the story you tell yourself and others to "I accept these foods willingly and lovingly, without any negative or ill effects!" This may sound cheesy, and I didn't buy into this stuff at first, and once I did, I still procrastinated on practicing these simple techniques, but after implementing them in my life, I realized the power my thoughts had and felt it was necessary to share, so you can try it for yourself.

Your thoughts can often lie to you. You do not have to believe every thought that enters your mind, nor do you have to act on every thought that comes to mind. You always have a choice and always question your thoughts. If you don't think or question your thoughts, they become automatic or "they just occur" without being correct. Thoughts that are bothering you, that are negative, that are judgmental towards other people or yourself, that create fear and anxiety in you, that think others are judging you, that produce guilt, that blame, that overthink, that are talking you out of pursuing your dreams, thoughts telling you that you are not smart enough or worth it, thoughts telling you how ugly/fat/worthless you are, these thoughts you would probably feel much better without.

When you notice, acknowledge, or reflect upon your thoughts, you can become aware to see if they are helping or hurting you. If they are hurting you, you can talk back to the thoughts and create resistance; resistance usually is uncomfortable at first, but uncomfortable feelings usually result in change, and change ultimately is used for growth, and without growth in our existence, we are dead and not *living*.

You cannot stop your thoughts, but you can train your mind to create more positive thoughts (positive thoughts that are accurate, true, and in line with your reality, since negative thoughts are usually lies you are telling yourself). The truth can set you free. If a negative and nagging thought persists, telling you "You are so fat, you are a whale! You're so pudgy, it's not attractive nor sensual," you sit with that thought, maybe write it down, and ask yourself, "Is that thought true?" "Can I absolutely know it is true?" "How do I react when I believe that thought (mentally and physically)?" "Who would I be without the thought? Or how would I feel if I didn't have the thought?" This is a technique called "The Work" used by Byron Katie in her book *Loving What Is*.

Every thought we have, negative or positive, our body can hear the thought and believes it to be true. The body reacts accordingly, which is why some people get physical symptoms, such as stomachaches, headaches, or eye twitches, when people are emotionally stressed or upset; when someone gets excited or feels love, their body feels energized, they feel a fluttering stomach, or their heart rate speeds up. As Dr. Amen said, "Some people have no idea that the source of their suffering is within their own synapses." Sometimes, our thoughts create unnecessary stress and suffering.

Although it's great to think positively, it's not always going to be positive in life. It's just not possible; that's the duality of nature. With positive, there must come negative; we try not to let the negative times or thoughts take over; rather, we just acknowledge them when they are present and feel it; don't run away from the negative thoughts. Trying to be positive, or forcing positive affirmations when you're feeling down in the slums of self-loathing is just another way of running away from something, rather than dealing with it, and it just won't be believable.

It's hard to jump straight from feeling unsatisfied and hateful towards our body into thinking we're perfect and sexy-beasts. Because we will not be 100% happy or confident all the time. No, why? We're humans and that's just part of the human experience. So, if you want a fairytale of perfect happiness and positivity with no sadness or emotions, ever, then you just can't be a human. Try to incorporate more authentic and believable statements, such as "I'm learning to appreciate myself and body the way I am" "I'm realizing I'm more than just my external appearance" "I'm acknowledging the fact that I feel healthier and happier in my nourished body, compared to my malnourished body, despite the aesthetic difference" or "I'm changing the distorted beliefs and fat phobic thoughts I've had about my health and weight" or "I'm learning to not be so obsessive and fearful around food and restrictions."

Also, once I changed MY story in my head....the one that told myself and everyone around me daily that "I react to all these foods, I feel ill other than eating fruits and veggies, I feel guilt, shame, disgust, weak from eating the foods other than raw," I changed this internal message I was telling my mind and body to "I am fine, my body can digest these foods perfectly fine, these foods are not poisoning me, they are not going to kill me or hurt me, I am healthy, I am strong." It may be hard to believe (or not), but it really helps! Your body truly hears everything your mind is telling it, true or not, and over time, it manifests as our reality. Your Brain makes happen what it focuses on. We need to take action and change things slowly in our diet to build our bodies again, but it doesn't hurt and will help so much to change these internal thoughts as a supplement.

On the note of changing limiting internal belief patterns and stories... It's worth mentioning meditation, mindfulness, prayer, visualization, or whatever you want to call it... All these practices are very helpful. Whether you're into it or not, it's highly recommended, and worth trying to see how good it feels to calm your mind and quiet that internal chatter. With meditation, guided meditation, prayer, or any of these practices, you can visualize and focus on changing your negative behaviors associated with your disordered eating habits or negative body image, and imagine what it feels like to be healed, healthy, confident, and how good it feels to be living a normal life.

Change your focus for a moment from the negative issues you are facing to what you have to look forward to and the positive changes soon to come. Feel these positive changes as if they were your reality right now. Visualize and mediate on how real and good these changes feel, as if they are your reality. Imagine eating your "fear foods" free of fear and feeling energized, happy, and free of negative reactions to the foods. Imagine yourself moving your body or engaging in fun physical activities for joy only, and free from stressful and obsessive thoughts around the body movement. Imagine loving your weight gain, your rebalanced body, and feeling fantastic with your nourished and beautiful healthy body. Feel the feelings of freedom full recovery has given you, the health you've regained, the 'jolly joy' you've reclaimed, and the relationships you've mended or made new. Try your hardest to believe it.

Close your eyes and take deep long breaths, slowly, into the deepest parts of your diaphragm and extending your lower belly. Deep breathing activates the Prefrontal Cortex of the brain, which is the "thinking part of the brain." This will not just allow you to think, but to think properly, and make more well-rounded decisions. Deep breathing also calms your sympathetic nervous system, which is your stress reactions or what puts you in "fight or flight" mode. We want to shift into the parasympathetic nervous system to help calm the nerves, which, yep, you guessed it, the deep breathing helps initiate. The parasympathetic nervous system controls your resting state, relaxation, and digestive responses. When the parasympathetic system is dominant and commanding, your breath slows, your heart rate drops, the blood vessels relax causing your blood pressure to lower, and your body is put into a state of calmness and healing. This is only a tidbit of what the breath can do. See the power of breath?!

Do this practice for about 10 minutes, up to 30 minutes, or longer or even shorter if you so desire. Try it in the morning upon rising and/or right before meals and during the meal with bites to make sure you're not tense and stressed while eating. As you move throughout your journey, with these visuals in place and assisting you, the real-life actions will appear to happen more smoothly as you persist. Doing these exercises brings more oxygen, blood, and nutrients to the brain. You also create more neural pathways in the brain to help you do the things in real life. You are prepping and practicing for the real thing in your mind.

After this mediation practice, write down 3 things you value and love most about yourself. This will help to rewire and restructure your brain patterns, your thoughts, and your beliefs. These will then affect and manifest as our feelings and then into our *actions*. We can change all these aspects to substitute negative and limiting patterns for positive and empowering patterns; from fear into courage, from scarcity into abundance, from insecurity to confidence, from unfaithfulness to trust, and so on.

Typically, when one is entrapped in habits of restrictive and disordered eating behaviors, they lose their sense of self and other important aspects of themselves, such as: personality, values, character, etc. which makes them unique, likable, attractive, etc. They replace and limit their value, worth, and likability, strictly on their external appearance, from being the skinniest, or being the fittest, or being the prettiest, or having the best make-up/hair, etc.

You may fear your true self getting rejected, because you've leaned on these external aspects for so long to feel accepted or desired that you might run away from rekindling your inner self again. I can assure you, it is safe to be *yourself* again, and it is liberating to reconnect and be able to express your authentic inner self again. It's worth taking the time to find this suppressed part of you again; trust me. These Guided meditations, silent meditations, moving meditations, prayer, etc. will help you to sit with yourself for once, get into your body, unable to run away anymore, and be without your distractions. You can face the reality and the masks/acts, what's fake and what's real, to filter through and find your truth again. Do not underestimate this practice!

Another suggestion is finding a trusted therapist that specializes in Cognitive Behavioral Therapy (CBT). This therapy is the most effective for people with restrictive eating disorders and will most likely ensure you have a complete and life-long recovery. This treatment will help rewire the dysfunctional and distorted thought processes and help to generate new neuronal pathways to overcome your ED neurotransmitter pathways, weakening them, and reversing them. Any psychological support to put a stop to fear or anxiety that may tempt you to restrict after eating is very useful if you can't seem to break the cycle yourself.

BODY IMAGE RE-COVERY

This is a patient, long, and slow process to recover a normal "diet" and lifestyle and positive body image, which is just as much of a process, in which both are equally important, and you can't really have one without the other. It is a process, and just like the diet recovery approach, acceptance of your body will take persistence, and you will most likely encounter relapses and reversion back to old thoughts. You hammer that head of the inner critic that pops up in new holes every time you succeed at stomping it, just like that game Whac-A-Mole, and you keep moving forward, without feeling defeat and the desire to give up.

Body shaming and dissatisfaction with appearance are the fuels that drive all the madness of dieting, restricting, obsessing, overtraining, and the binge-purge behaviors. The real problem is that many people don't put the time or effort into developing body acceptance and love for their body at their current size in the present moment, even when being aware this is a crucial part of the process. This is because they've either learned or created habits to object to embracing body acceptance.

99% of women's "food problems" are typically disguised as stemming from body image issues. The constant societal pressures (on women, in particular) to be thin is actually what creates weight issues with chronic dieting and only eating "clean."

Has your self-love been determined by something external, such as fitting into a pair of skinny jeans or the number of compliments you receive from friends, family, or strangers, or whether you hit a caloric deficit, or hit a certain amount of workouts that week? Maybe you bought into the bullshit out there that you're not worthy until you meet these specific standards? Maybe it's time to take a break from the daily scale weigh-ins, the body pinching, the mirror flexing, the selfie taking, and the checking of social media likes, hearts, and compliments. It makes the process a whole hell of a lot easier to take your focus away from the modern diet culture and beauty demands, by taking your energy and attention away from things that make you focus on your own external appearance and feel crappy and insecure about yourself, such as social media feed, magazines, movies, and TV.

And this does not just go for women. The diet culture and beauty standards have created unsustainable ideals for men to live up to as well. These unsustainable standards make men feel unworthy and less desirable if they are not exactly the shadow puppet of those one-size-fits-all standards. If they aren't perfectly ripped and have eight pack abs or biceps bigger than our noggins, they aren't as "sexy." I know many boys and men who are both openly and privately striving to recover from restrictive eating disorders, including anorexia, bulimia, overtraining, and all the other physical and mental damage and programming instilled in them. They feel no female will ever love them because they don't look like the Calvin Klein model or Thor. I also see too many young kids struggling with dieting and body dysmorphia, even at ages 11 and 12, for goodness sake! How unfortunate, right?

So, let me ask this; what does body shaming really do for you? Does it really benefit you? Would you survive without it? Fuck ya you would, and you'd be much happier without those thoughts and comments to yourself. So, if you're going to look the way you do right now, or forever, you might as well be nice to yourself, and learn to love and accept yourself, so you can have a pleasant and joyful experience, rather than a shitty shit-storm of an experience along the way. Body shaming is not helping you; it's only hurting you and perpetuating the disordered eating cycle.

Learn to love what you have at this moment. Be patient with this process. Having positive body image is determined by the foundational belief you are enough, just as you are. Stop comparing yourself to others around you or in the media or on your Facebook friends page or the Instagram page you follow religiously. These stories people post of themselves on social media is only a fraction of the picture. You never know what makes up the rest of their days, thoughts, actions, feelings, relationships, etc. You cannot assume their life is a perfect paradise of perfection. Realize, they are human, just like you, that either worked their ass off to get to where they are, tears, sweat, suffering, and obstacles along the way, or their life is a walking prison and they hate everything about their lifestyle, even with all the wealth, smiles, "perfect body," and/or friends they try to show off in their virtual social media life. Why would people post all the bad photos of themselves, or the times extremely boring or when something bad happened? People want to show their best to impress others, not show their weakness. They want to be liked and desired, just as much as you may do.

Here are suggestions on how to engage in social media while protecting yourself:

- For starters, unsubscribe to all the people preaching restriction of any sort and act in a way that what they're doing is superior to everyone else or their lifestyle is the 'only' way.

-Replace those folks and follow people that talk about non-restrictive behaviors, empowerment, body-acceptance, mental health work, and positivity. Listen to podcasts or watch YouTube videos that talk about these same things.

-Follow accounts that aren't posting "#foodporn" all day or people who aren't posting booty shots or ab photos, or before and after pictures, or aren't talking about macronutrients or "fear foods" all day long.

-Follow yoga accounts that aren't crazily skinny and/or ripped, but are perhaps considered "plus size" (because what people consider plus size most of the time are just NORMAL in real life); follow models that promote body acceptance or 'plus size' models, (which usually are just *normal* size 8-10 women that the media deems as plus size because they aren't stick thin anorexics) or any size , skinny or big, (no skinny shaming either!) as long as they aren't sharing restrictive disordered madness. Just try to follow different shapes/types of bodies, kinds of people in the media/social media.

-Follow people who aren't afraid to post their true selves, the ones that get themselves out there and are not "done up" all the time, with crazy moles/birthmarks/lisps/lazy eyes/crazy laughs/an awkward manners/etc. They show up as them, don't care, and know they are more than just what they "appear to be externally," and many people are drawn to them for it! Not to say, being "done up" or skinny is now to be demonized, but come on, you get the point, right? Follow and appreciate everyone!

Don't know where to find these body positivity accounts or non-restrictive food accounts? I know I didn't know where to find good ones, so let me help with a few recommendations:

Instagram: Denisebidot, Recovrywarriors, theashleygraham, curvy.be, khrystyana, jessraeking, positivebodyimage, recoverytodaymagazine, katemareeobrian, eatingpsychology, thefuckitdiet, projectheal, jessicaearle_model, jennatilemile, beating_binge_eating, summerinannen, ifd_bodies.

There is a worldwide fat phobia going around these days, but there is a huge shift leaning towards a movement of body acceptance as well. There is also a lack of body diversity in the media of our modern culture. When you look in magazines or tv advertisements, can you find any models with a similar body or body parts to yours, such as legs, stomach, arms, skin, or butt? If you can, it's rare and is definitely not the majority, but the minority. *"Challenging stereotypes that we have about certain body types and celebrating all bodies is necessary to having a good body image. There are LOTS of women (and men) working towards breaking these standards and showing that you can be worthy at any size."* (Summer Innanen)

While it takes time and effort to get to a point where you can accept and love yourself for what you are and what you have at this point in your life, it's attainable and well worth the investment, instead of continuing to hate yourself and critique yourself day in and day out, because that's what we've been conditioned to do in all honesty.

Why do we continue to inflict self-harm in such a way as not accepting and loving ourselves? It seems so much more pleasant without it, doesn't it? Why is it hard to break the negative self-hate thoughts? Why is it harder to develop self-love, self-acceptance, and empowerment? *It's familiar misery.* We are comfortable with it. Comfortable and familiar are easier. We like easy. Challenge is hard and work. HA! We are surrounded by the media from the day we're born and the day we are exposed to the world. But you know what's better; challenging ourselves and our belief systems to endure the growing pains and reap the magical rewards of self-love, acceptance, and freedom. And that empowering love trumps all other negativity, and we step into a whole other dimension of living.

Your body image may not be the best nor throughout recovery, but months 6-8, the one year mark, or even two or more years in, of working diligently on your body image, more or less, you'll get to a point where you'll be less prone to *act* on those negative self/body thoughts. You'll realize relapsing into restricting won't work nor is it sustainable and will only set you back in your progression. You'll develop the desire to accept the body as it is and not have the urge to change or control it, because you know now the lengths you have to go to and the things in life you have to sacrifice, mentally and physically, to maintain it if you go back.

Loving your body does not mean your life will now be perfect with no days of feeling down and not feeling sexy or attractive, loving your appearance 24/7. Like everything else, our emotions and feelings ebb and flow from days to weeks, to months, to years. Having a core belief and understanding that all bodies, including genders, sizes, shapes, races, ages, personalities, etc., yours included, are valuable, irreplaceable, and worthy, helps you stay strong within all of the ebbs and flows.

Developing body confidence and total self-acceptance does not mean you have to stop all efforts towards your external appearance. You don't have to totally stop wearing any makeup, doing your hair, wearing your favorite fancy clothes, or ever shaving again, unless you want to! It just means you are detaching your total self-worth and value coming from only your external appearance and buying into the culture demands and messages that teach us we're

Damn The Diets

not good enough unless we meet these certain superficial standards.

Don't force yourself into "body love" if you hate your body right this moment. Start with body acceptance, just trying to get to a point of being neutral and where you're okay with your body, not hating it but not loving it. Your flaws, your scars, your whatever it is you don't like about your body is a part of your story and your uniqueness that have made you into who you are today.

In a world that tells you you have to have one particular type of body, it's hard to look at your body and think yours is just as beautiful and desirable right off the bat, because the rest of the world isn't telling you this or giving you the space to develop this either. The rest of the world is saying you have to force yourself to be like this; this is how to be and how you have to have your body. So, start with acceptance. I'm grateful to have gotten this insight from Summer Innanen's work.

We are trying to get away from the perfectionist mindset, and with body acceptance, perfectionism makes us feel the need to have to love every part of ourselves totally, and this has set us up for feelings of inadequacy and failure. Embracing all the pieces of yourself, including the not so good, the good, and the whatever parts, is crucial to letting go of the perfection quest.

Wherever you are, be willing to gain or lose weight, and be comfortable with the results, from nourishing your body with what it needs to heal and be healthy. If you gain weight, your body NEEDED it whether you think you need to or not; your body knows best. If you lose weight effortlessly and you *feel* healthy, that too was needed, and your body was *ready* for it. If your body lets go of any weight, by doing what's recommended to recover, heal, and find your balance in this book, then that is the only healthful way I know for it to occur. A healthful weight will be achieved by itself, without your help, or you forcing anything as you go through recovery; be patient and let it all balance out naturally. Do not try to control the process; be patient and accept the process and know whatever happens needed to happen. The health you gain far surpasses the weight composition fluctuations you deal with in the process. Feeling happy, healthy, joyful, and giddy is so much more gratifying than a number on the scale, a pudge on your body when you sit down, the thigh gap you look to as a gold medal, or the six pack of your conditioned dreams. Your weight and aesthetic obsessions are honestly a waste of your precious time!

Spending your valuable and limited life here on earth trying to obtain unrealistic goals to look like a supermodel, or a physique/bikini competitor, or your guru, or whatever your goal is cannot be obtained and sustained. I've been to both extremes; both were living prisons in their own unique way. I was stick skinny at a couple of points and was ripped for fitness modeling and bikini competing and no exaggeration, every aspect of my physical health, mental health, and my life was falling apart in different ways at each point. It is soul sucking, energy draining, emotionally taxing, relationship breaking, and everything ruining, and I wouldn't go back if I was paid a million dollars to manipulate and deplete my body and lose all joy again or for another sponsorship or modeling contract ever again. The way I feel now, the freedom I have now, even when carrying more weight than those days (normal weight and muscle) outweighs that lifestyle by a million percent.

"The more time you give to the pursuit of "attaining a certain body image" the more of an obsession it becomes and the more it takes over your life and thoughts.

Stop living life by "what if" and start living life by "what is" and live it with joy." -Cambry.

The media targets our desire to attain a certain persona and profile "type" that is unrealistically unreachable and is continually bombarding us with the exact triggers that continue this dark cycle. No matter what goals you accomplish in life, if you can never accept yourself from the start (where you're at now, most likely) when you get to the end goal, you still won't be satisfied and will still want. You need to develop self-acceptance NOW, or enjoy your life NOW, or be happy with what you have NOW to appreciate what you may obtain.

"This logic promises that when the weight-obsessed individual finally achieves a certain weight, she/he will be satisfied with the appearance of her/his body. But this is a false promise. An eating-disordered culture functions by making people deeply dissatisfied with their appearance, no matter what that appearance happens to be." Paul Campos; The Obesity Myth

It's not what you don't have that makes you feel bad about yourself, because in reality, with all the riches in the world, all the friends in the world, with the most perfect body in the world, the focus will turn into some other insecurity to perseverate on, whether it's your hair, you birthmark, your toes, your nose, your scoliosis, your sweaty palms, your friends, your partner, your car, your shirt, you'll find something to direct your focus towards. Instead, focus your energy and time and thoughts into a new hobby, new positive relationships, and new healthy progressive endeavors.

Get yourself out of your mind for a while and out into reality more. Don't get dragged back into the self-perpetuating negative thought cycle. It takes time, but with persistence and resilience, it can and will be done for you; just be patient with yourself.

All these people we idolize, models, average IG peeps, fitness accounts, etc. look super happy and energized and as if they have a perfect life that's full of unicorns, rainbows, and exponential happiness, but behind the scenes are irritable bitches (yes, guys included), who are lacking energy and facing many major physical problems, or if not just yet, will so eventually.

"Dropping the pursuit of weight loss isn't about giving up, it's about moving on. When you make choices because they help you feel better, not because of their presumed effect on your weight, you maintain them over the long run." Linda Bacon, Health at Every Size.

You cannot fix your insecurities or general problems by losing weight, or looking a certain way or attaining certain external material goods. This is only fixed from a feeling within of acceptance and love for yourself. If these external things or weight loss come with your lifestyle changes and positive actions and behaviors, then great! But if they don't, oh well, everything is still all groovy! The whole goal of researching and attempting to adopt healthful and nutritious habits is simply to feel better, so you can live life to the fullest, accomplish and attain your dreams and aspirations. The goal is not to be the perfect puppet and follower of the nutrition guru or pop star. But, we are human, and we are imperfectly perfect, and with the law of duality comes both ups and downs. We cannot let the downs totally outweigh the ups and demoralize our lives forever, but just know this too will pass and continue with life unaffected permanently.

Here's a tip; try changing your language and the emotions you relate and identify with the words, such as "fat" and "skinny" or "toned" and "big." There are very degrading stereotypes out there these days around our bodies, and we take them on and believe them. What I mean by this is "fat or big" has been associated with being unhealthy, a failure, lazy, shameful, unsuccessful, non-sexy, frustrated, miserable, and uncomfortable, while "skinny, toned, or lean" has been associated with success, confidence, worthiness, sexy, popularity, happiness, beauty, and pride. These unrealistic standards stemming from the beauty industry and diet culture make us develop fear around gaining weight and worship thinness. Having this mindset prevents us from ever feeling confident and accepting of our bodies unconditionally.

So, when you redevelop your self-love and acceptance and overcome your disordered eating and want to adopt certain healthful lifestyle habits, do not do it so strategically, but more so because you truly want to because it makes you feel good and that's it. Nothing further than that. If you feel stress and obsession creeping back in, back off the lifestyle changes, and do only what helps you not hurts you.

Weight is so much more than the number and indicator of level of health or an unhealthy state. Just because one seems to be "overweight" (well, to our conditioned and blurred judgment) does not deem them as unhealthy and disease ridden. Weight is not the determiner of health. When looking at an active heavier person to a thin but sedentary person, the heavier person is most often healthier. To diet and take drugs and appetite suppressants, diuretics, laxatives, abuse exercise, etc. in efforts to make ourselves thin, we end up contributing and causing us to be overweight and health lacking. We are not solving the problem of "being fat" but contributing to the disease itself. Periodic and recurring dieting is the best way for future weight gain.

"The belief that being fat is unhealthy is false. In fact, in the United States, at age 70 and above, those with Level 1 obesity (BMI of 30-35) have the lowest rates of degenerative disease and greatest longevity statistics, particularly if you are physically fit and don't cycle your weight (meaning yo-yo diet)." Matt Stone Diet Recovery.

"Being overweight is associated with numerous diseases, but we have to understand that correlation does not mean causation. Similarly, if a dog goes outside, and it starts raining, it's correlated, yes, but does it mean the dog caused the rain? Today we don't actually even know if diabetes comes after a person has gained weight or if the person's weight gain is a symptom of diabetes, as surgeon and nutrition researcher Peter Attia has suggested. There is a big difference. No one truly knows which comes first, the illness or the weight gain." (Oras, Elisa. BrainwashED)

Very few people are naturally 18.5-20 BMI. A BMI of 25-30 in the medical world is technically 'overweight' but it does not indicate health. Train your body not just to survive for looks; have fun, love what you're doing, and eat and savor the foods you love. Find what you love to do and what works for you, and the results will follow.

Chronic conditions typically considered to be corresponding to obesity are seen at all weights. Even the Journal of the American Medical Association study found "Overweight was not associated with excess mortality." (Stephan Guyenet, The Body Fat Set Point).

"Many are encouraged by their treatment teams to stop gaining weight and "maintain" their weight as soon as they reach the lowest part of the "healthy range" being 18.5-20 BMI. Yet, 70% of women are naturally going to

fall between BMI of 21-27 with more than half at 23, 24, or 25. Fundamentally, the optimal weight range for lowest incidence of ill health and death is actually BMI of 25-30. The minimum guidelines for recovery are, on average, what non-restricting, weight-stable, individuals in your category consume to maintain their weight and health. You gain weight through all the phases of recovery because the metabolism is suppressed; that energy went to weight gain and repair. Once you are recovered the energy now goes to day-to-day functions (all the neuroendocrine systems that had been on hold up to that point).

You gain on recovery amounts and then you maintain on right about the same amount.

Once you stop gaining weight, then you can also depend on your hunger cues to keep you eating what your body needs to maintain your health and weight for the rest of your life. Unfortunately, many will be encouraged to restrict under the auspices of maintenance of your weight and health. Restriction of food intake will always precipitate relapse. Restrictive Eating Disorders are chronic conditions, not ever to be totally cured of the condition. You can enjoy a complete and even permanent remission, but it requires of you that you never restrict your food sources or intake. Our society suffers such severe anxiety over obesity and believes wrongly that both food intake and exercise determine the appearance and onset of obesity, that many health care providers will encourage patients to be careful about their intake and get back to exercising in this phase for all the wrong reasons.

Keep in mind that a disproportionate number of those in the nutritional sciences are also on the restrictive eating disorder spectrum." (EDInstitue.org)

You don't maintain your weight; your body does and only your body decides what your optimal weight set point is, not you, or other doctors, or me, or family, or anyone else. Your body will always go back to its natural set weight point no matter how much dieting and restriction you do. It's also important to realize that, if you've had an eating disorder throughout your early teenage years, and you finally recover, your natural set-weight point can and most likely will be higher than your set-weight point when you were 14. It's just part of the maturity process, growing up from a teenage girl and into a woman with curves, boobs, hips, thighs, and a booty. These are needed for natural reproduction and biological purposes to get the female body ready for pregnancy and being a mother of a child. Or a boy into a man who is stronger, hairier, and less scrawny like the boy.

So, there's no need to strive to be as stick thin as a 13-year-old anymore. If your eating disorder(s) occurred in adulthood, or both teenage and adulthood for many years, you may be unaware of what your healthy set-weight is. You don't have to know what it is; your body has it covered. It'll get there whether you know it or not, and perhaps, it is better you don't know so you're not trying to control the outcome of being weight restored. If you maintain a certain weight when restricting, dieting, or during a vigorous work out regimen and it's hard for you to stick with it healthfully or not able to sustain it without cravings, then that is definitely not your body's natural, set-weight! You will have to continue to restrict and diet just to maintain the weight you got, and when you stop, your body will go back to its set-weight point and then some.

A huge step in truly gaining body acceptance is identifying your degrading *theories* for your body, and challenging the validity of those beliefs. If you think "loving yourself as is will keep you fat and sick," ask yourself this: has hating and degrading your body and nitpicking at all your flaws all these years resulted in any permanent weight loss? Has it successfully "motivated" you to sustain these so-called healthful behaviors around food and exercise in the long-term? I'm assuming no. Body acceptance and self-love is one of the top, if not the most important step, for you to work on if you want to have a healthy relationship with food again and to break free from the restrictive and shameful prison.

Do you feel like you could never love yourself at this or that certain weight, size, or shape? Honestly, what makes you think you'll finally be happy with yourself if you can't even master it now? Because once you get to your "dream" weight or size, it still won't be enough because you never worked on body love for yourself in the first place. So, when you've arrived at your new weight, you've arrived with your same negative and degrading mindset.

Do you think no one else will love you at this size? Is the real issue here, *fear of judgement by others?* Do you get compliments from others, but still don't *believe* them? It's not that others won't love you the way you are; this is more of a personal dysmorphic problem you have going on internally. You think others won't love you the way you are, because you don't love yourself the way you are. How you feel about your body is usually not what other people see. Just like how your best friend is always pointing out flaws or insecurities about themselves that you probably never noticed or cared about. Same goes with you; you are your own worst critic, amplifying the slightest details into the most monstrous catastrophes.

Loving yourself doesn't make you fat (or unhealthy), and hating yourself doesn't make you thin (or healthy). The fight against developing self-love or justifications we tell ourselves why we *shouldn't* love our bodies the way they are, are mostly every person's biggest struggle to overcome in re-mending their relationship with food.

I've gained weight, and I've lost weight since full recovery, but it's hardly noticeable; it's part of the ebb and flow of life. You're never going to be one way or one weight all the time. Everything fluctuates. You still can wear your jeans; they may be a little tight, but it's okay. Life and these things are never constant, so just go with it and not focus on it, nor think it's bad. You're still beautiful and living your life! When I have gained a few pounds here and there, I don't care anymore. I had fun! And I know it's not per-manent, and I know I'll gain more, but I also know that it will all balance out, and I look forward to the good times that come with it.

All the years I struggled with bingeing/restricting and hav-ing a severe body obsession, I was consumed with trying to be smaller, thinner, toner, leaner, and just overall "better" than I was despite any progress I made. I never thought freedom would come to mean that, when my weight fluc-tuates, it doesn't change how much love, value, or honor I experience or think about or treat myself differently. And I don't hold back, regardless of how my clothes fit that day. I continue to cherish and connect with my body, myself, and my loved ones. Whether those pants are looser or tighter than the last time I put them on, it doesn't really phase me. I'm no longer owned by the scale, or by my thighs, or by the flatness of my stomach. I want every person who struggles with their relationship with food and their body to have this freedom. It's freaking magical. It's a totally dif-ferent level of confidence and a totally different level of freedom. And a different level of self-love. And it allows me to be freed up to help more people.

If you choose or have had a team who shows signs of anxi-ety around weight and body image, or project it onto you, they should not be your support system and you should seek support from another team; even if they were supportive initially, this will indefinitely not allow full and sustainable recovery, but provoke relapse(s).

If you have a dietician or nutritionist helping you with food ideas and meal plans, soak up the information for meal plans that resonate with you. Go along with your recommended intake for recovery, so you can avoid receiving advice that will lessen the chance of success for your recovery. Have someone who specializes or understands the fundamentals for restrictive eating disorder recovery. You cannot have a therapist or nutritionist that inflicts their personal fears as well as "healthy" and restrictive food beliefs on their clients, rather than encouraging and supporting them each to find their own way and state of homeostasis that best suits them. This is crucial for your success long term.

Know that a healthy and pleasurable life is a byproduct for having a healthy body and mind. Your focus should be "getting healthy" not having a "perfect life." *Your version* of what the best life will look like for *you* will come as you heal and nurture your body and mind. If you are unhappy with your body, realize it is better, healthier, and safer to do nothing than to exhaust yourself through restricting, starving, over exercising, and dieting. Start thinking of the long-term effects and do not live for the short-term high, or in this case, the "perfect body" or the "perfect diet." If you go for the "quick fix" of restricting, dieting, or over-exercising, your body will fight back in the long term, and you'll be left even more unhappy with all the extra weight gain, the physical and mental side effects, the binging, and the lowered metabolism.

Stop trying on old clothes that once fit you. Donate your clothes; if they fit you during your disordered eating days, they shouldn't fit you in the future! It can be a trigger when clothes don't fit you, even though this is a great sign you're restoring your weight and on your way to full recovery! What your weight and clothing sizes were prior is not what you want to be at again. If they still fit you in recovery, *you are not recovering!*

Most people during recovery tend to live in sweats, oversized sweaters, loose dresses, or just anything loose, stretchy, and comfortable. You may not even recognize yourself in the mirror, because your body has changed so dramatically, or so you think, after being so skinny, depleted, and starved for however long. You adapt to seeing yourself as a certain way when in starvation. So, when you regain some weight and retain water, this can be shocking and rather concerning. Don't worry; your sense of image will catch up with you, and you may even accept and love your new curves as I did.

I have a HUGE new appreciation for the differences of female (and male) bodies; curves in specific for women, and men who are not super bulky and unrealistically huge and striated. I know how much it takes to get both huge and cut, in a male's situation, and get super thin as well as hard and bulky in females. I look up to women of any age, who have beautiful and voluptuous curves and flaunt it, and think of them as true female goddesses that walk the earth. I look to guys who are confident in themselves, not insecure because they aren't as ripped or big as the guys promoted to us via the media or on the stage. There was this girl in my hometown I always admired as my dream girl goddess body; she had badass curves and was the epitome of a female goddess (in *my* eyes). Before though, I was so programmed to think any curves looked or meant you were fat or chubby. That has changed heaps. I don't necessarily think it's beautiful, all these women starving themselves to get 13-year-old bodies.

Another note, I did not like losing my butt and curves AT ALL during my fitness and orthorexic eating disorder days. My butt cheeks turned into flat saggy pancakes that were floppy and not healthy looking in the least bit. I always loved having a butt, and being as skinny as I was, even in the fitness competition days, was not what I wanted, and it even made me very frustrated and insecure. When I got my butt back in recovery, and then some, I honestly loved it! I loved my new hips and butt.

What I had to focus more on was my mental state; although I enjoyed my new curves, I still had the media and society right around the corner telling me those curves are not what I want, and I need to be skinnier to be "healthy" and "fit" even though I felt the healthiest I'd felt in years! It was a battle in my mind; one part was accepting and happy, the other was insecure and judgmental. Over time, not overnight, the battle leaned more towards the accepting and loving side, and eventually overpowered the negative thoughts. It became less frequent that the unhappiness side of the battle came into my mind, and I landed in a place of truly not caring what others thought, but really how I felt.

What once was my ideal body type was what I did not want, but instead wanted the total opposite. If a lady is naturally super skinny, then that's just as beautiful, but it's the fact that if it's not your natural body type, that's just what it looks like, unnatural and not as attractive as the natural body set point would for them. I also had a dear and close friend back then, and she was stick thin effortlessly; no matter what she did or ate, she stayed very slim, but she was just as beautiful in my eyes, as these other thick and curvy girls I thought were gorgeous. She was like a fairy princess with no makeup in the early hours of the morning and had such a sweet caring soul. The unfortunate part is, both gals got mocked for their weight and appearance. So honestly, no matter what size you are, no matter what you look like, you're always going to have haters out there that will find something negative to say about you! It's a lose-lose situation if you're in this people pleasing pickle. It's near impossible to get everyone to like you. You can never satisfy everyone, so why not just be happy pleasing yourself with what makes you feel sane, happy, and full of life? Whoever else is pleased along the way, appreciate them and focus on the supportive ones, but know it's not *for* them. You're not here in life to please other people nor win everyone's approval anyway; there is so much more to life.

Summer Innanen, author of Body Image Remix, explains the people pleasing pickle beautifully:
"Fitting in and being accepted is "safe"—it protects us from being an outcast and reliving the pain of our childhood when we were called last to be on a team or not invited to scrapbook fuzzy stickers with Heather- Anne at recess. When we're so focused on winning the praise of others and looking like we have it all figured out, we don't allow ourselves to really be seen. It's impossible to be who you really are when all your concerns are tied up in what other people will think. It took me a long time to realize I'd rather be someone's cotton candy ice cream than everyone's vanilla.
Disclaimers are for legal documents, not people! Being unapologetic means letting go of what other people think and letting your true self roar.
What's one thing you want to be more unapologetic about? Speaking your mind? Wearing what you want? Eating what you truly desire? For starters, pick one thing to actively be more unapologetic about."

People pleasing... isn't that what all this is about? You are trying to please others; you want to please society and what it expects you to be, to get them to like and accept you. Is it, perhaps, because you don't love or accept yourself, and therefore need these feelings of acceptance or reassurance from others outside of you to fill the void you are holding yourself from feeling? When in reality, the most gratifying and real feeling of love and acceptance must first come from within, from yourself and for yourself, before anyone else can truly and genuinely give these feelings to you in return. Ever hear that saying, "You must first love yourself, before you can truly love another?" Well, it's the truth. Our external world reflects ourselves. How you see yourself and what you think of yourself is how you show up in the world. If you love and accept yourself, you have a better chance at being a better human in society, a better parent, spouse, sibling, cousin, coworker, or friend.

People are more sensitive than you think. Authenticity, self-confidence, and self-love is powerful. Change the way you see yourself and have compassion for yourself, and things around you will change for the better; you'll even attract more loving people into your life.

Ever been around that person you can't say is the most beautiful or fit person in the world, but their charm and self-confidence is what you just love and melt over when around them? Everyone gravitates to them in the room. They are fun, eccentric, and non-judgmental. You feel comfortable around them, right? They are the definition of self-acceptance, and it's a beautiful thing. That's the place you should get before anything can change for a good healthy reason. On the other hand, you can be around someone who still is not the most beautiful person, but puts on an in-genuine fake persona, and when around them you feel insecure and not able to express yourself fully, or you feel they're just "why so serious?" Well, that's because, most often, they are insecure, devoid of self-love and acceptance, and therefore their down and out energy rubs off on those around them. Anyway, we'll talk more about this in the Body Image Section of the book.

Start to look at and appreciate *all* the beautiful body shapes of both men and women, who are doing amazing things in this world, and don't have that same body you see on every billboard, movie, magazine cover, and advertisement. Look at the real superheroes of our world, serving the people on our planet, helping our fellow patrons, and dedicated to the cause. These people may be: hairdressers, lawyers, nurses, healers, the person who always makes you smile at your local grocery store, charity workers helping the less fortunate, that person that made you laugh on the plane, that elder that gave you helpful words of wisdom, the singer that creates your favorite music, the model that inspires you to feel confident and loving to your body and self, the family member that never tries to 'change' anyone but always accepts you for you, and whatever other typical person that doesn't have the stereotypical body type you see all over the media.

Because we've been programmed to see the same body over and over since a very young age, we think that's the only body that's acceptable, and that's the body we should and need to have. Apparently, that's the 'best body,' even when that's only one type of body when there's supposed to be many and much diversity amongst us. It's just another way of conformity of the populace. It's just the body type the media wants you to think you need to have so you buy their products, their programs, their supplements, etc., and become dependent on them if you ever 'need' to lose weight again, because the cycle is, you will gain it all back and more if you fall into this diet and body shaming trap to look a certain way. We need to embrace our uniqueness. Just like there's no snowflakes that look alike, we too, are all unique human snowflakes, if you will. Anything in nature is unique, flowing, and different; every-thing man-made is mostly conformed, rigid, and with less diversity.

CONSIDER THIS...

Everyone with an ED develops certain eating disorder *behaviors*, in which they help to feed the disordered eating cycle. These need to be brought to your attention, so you can actively try to stop them. This is hard to do, just like any old habit, but if you're persistent, it will happen, and the payoff will be exponential.

Things I'm referring to are behaviors such as:
- constantly checking your body in the mirror
- pinching at fat in certain areas on your body
- constantly embarking on cleanses or fasts (water, juice, etc.), or intermittent fasting
- worrying about food combining
- worrying about eating foods in a certain order
- chugging water before meals
- obsessively watching YouTube nutrition videos
- calculating and tracking calories and macronutrients in your head or on calorie counting aps/websites at every meal (these calorie-calculations are clinically proven to underestimate your actual energy requirements)
- weighing foods,
- measuring foods
- writing down everything you eat
- hiding your food or how much food you eat
- trying to eat zero- calorie/sugar/fat/carb products
- tweaking the diet to be low in anything (low-fat, low-carb, low-sugar)
- limiting of foods to eat small portions
- hoarding food
- impulsive spending and returning items
- crazy and obsessive amounts of exercising
- making up excuses as to why you can't go out and eat with loved ones or avoiding social outings (because you

don't want to miss your 5th meal or be tempted by the food or desert or worry if you'll have access to "clean and pure" food sources)

You get the idea, weird and abnormal behaviors.

These are learned behaviors though. You didn't always have them and just like you learned those negative behaviors, you can learn new positive habits and behaviors. If you consistently try to create positive habits, over time, these positive habits will override and take the place of the negative habits. Just like when you're trying to learn something new, whether it's riding a bike, learning new software, or learning new training, at first, it didn't feel like it came easily. It didn't feel natural. You feel uncomfortable and frustrated, sometimes almost to tears. You feel like you just want to give up, because it's new and something you need to learn. At first, it requires constant repetition; no habit is created overnight. It takes commitment, patience, practice, faith, and persistency. At first, it's not an automatic behavior, but it starts with the desire to want to change. Once you slowly learn these new skills, they become second nature, and you'll have those abilities for the rest of your life, if you keep a constant effort in practicing them. If you don't use it, you lose it. If you're not hyperaware, you can easily get sucked back into the media and societal pressures to feel bad about yourself, your life, and your eating patterns.

At some point, we've bought in to the lie of waiting until "we're ready" or "when we feel it's right," or "for the right time" for us to change our life. We think at some point we'll finally develop the courage or the confidence. There's so many people holding back from what they really want to achieve, because they think they're missing motivation. It's simply not true. Realize you're never going to wake up one day and finally *feel* ready to do the things that are tough or difficult or uncertain or scary or new. So, we need to stop waiting until the perfect moment or when you feel like it.

"We often put our life on hold until we've achieved a certain appearance or weight. This is such bullshit! You deserve to be your future badass self now!
Many women stall on doing the things they want to do in the body they have because they are paralyzed by the fear of dropping their perfectionist shield.
In order to be the woman you desire to be, you may put yourself in a vulnerable position where you are open to rejection, judgment, or possible emotional discomfort. There is this big cloud of the scary unknown waiting on the other side. This is the healthy kind of fear that will ignite radical changes in how we feel about ourselves. In order to get comfortable in our own skin, we have to lean into this particular type of fear and discomfort.
Stepping into our fears allows us to get more comfortable with living the life we want to have in the body we have." (Summer Innanen)

You are one decision away from a new and rewarding life. Just face the fear and uncomfortable feelings of change, and do it despite everything, everyone, and every thought that's screaming to you not to do what you truly want. Breaking free from the diet trends, the popular nutritional dogmas, the communities you've engrained yourself in, and the beliefs you've created or taken on requires this risk, to go against everything you've learned, but know it hasn't been working in your favor.

Try your best to let go of the ideal to be "perfect" and trying so hard to be the "purist." Make efforts to stop the paranoia of being anything less than perfect. This is not what life is about. Life is about being imperfect and learning from mistakes and experiences, and failing at things but trying again, and going with the ups and downs in life.

Damn The Diets

There is no perfect diet, except the one that suits YOUR needs and lifestyle best. There is no perfect body type, except the one you have, and you feel healthiest in.

It's time to live for something more. Your priorities must now change if you want change, and you must live life past an identity based solely on your aesthetic appearance, numbers on the scale, and fat you pinch between your fingers. It's time to break this unhealthy neurobiological condition and rewire your unhealthy mindset and behavior you adopted towards food and your body, back into a healthy relationship. Instead of classifying food as a threat, see food for what it truly is. It's fuel and nourishment for your body to be a healthy human being. Food is not your enemy; restriction, fear, and the disordered thoughts towards food and your body is. Learning and implementing these non-restrictive behaviors and habits around food improves the expression of an eating disorder within the mind and body.

INTOLERANCES... OR NOT?

Do you claim to be allergic to lactose, gluten, nuts, soy, eggs, etc.? Well, you're on the right track to becoming "breatharian" as you cut out every food we have to choose from as a species! (don't get any ideas, even the self-acclaimed "breatharians" have been caught eating FOOD! Remember, we can't change our physiology over night because it *sounds* appealing or convenient to us.)

So, if you cut gluten or lactose because you are a self-acclaimed (not clinically diagnosed) Celiac or intolerant to wheat or gluten, this may be your restrictive disorder's way of telling you, "you can't eat these foods." So, you cut out as many dense foods as possible to live on. There are far too many people claiming to be celiac, or gluten intolerant when they simply are not because they choose to follow the trend to be gluten-free. You may feel digestion problems when trying to eat these foods, but its most often *not* necessarily the fact you're intolerant to these foods, but 1 of 2 reasons: 1- you are physically reacting to the stress response because every time you eat these "fear foods" you are tense and scared, or you began to believe you were intolerant, so it wreaks havoc on your digestion or 2- you have cut these foods out for so long and weakened your digestion that when you try to introduce them back in, your digestion's capabilities are lowered, which creates digestive discomfort.

This was me. I cut out dairy and gluten and told myself a story that I developed a strong belief about, which led to every time I ate those foods, I would "react" with certain symptoms I then blamed on those foods, which supported my belief. The symptoms were real, but that's just how powerful the mind is and how real starvation consequences are on the body ruining the digestive organs and metabolism. I eventually got over both the stress and the belief I created for myself, changed my story and negative feelings I had towards these foods, consistently fed myself all these foods, and now, I eat these foods daily and do just fine with them. Just food for thought (pun definitely intended).

Give your body a decent chance to adjust and build up a tolerance for the foods you seem to react to. I reacted to almost every food other than fruit and raw veggies at first; if I would've quit because of my negative reactions, I would have never recovered! (IF you honestly have dietary allergies, and these are real ones that aren't just in your head, then avoid them and do so accordingly of course.)

"The intestine adjusts its enzymes within just a few weeks; usually it only takes 2 weeks to have a complete adaptation of the digestive enzymes. But until your intestine has adjusted its enzymes to a new kind of diet, much of that food is going to be undigested, and it will feed bacteria rather than feeding the person. And the strange new growth of bacteria will produce lots of chemicals that can be toxic and allergenic. So, if a person isn't used to eating vegetables, and they eat vegetables, they'll often get a sore throat and runny nose, sore joints, headaches, and so on. Much of the food sensitivities issues is just adapting too suddenly to a diet; failing to adapt when they change, because they do it too suddenly.

Even if a person does have lactose intolerance from a lactase deficiency, tests have found that if they drink a cup of milk per meal, or less, they don't have the diarrhea that could be produced by drinking a pint of milk on an empty stomach. And even if they have had biopsies that show a deficiency of the lactase enzyme, that can be induced in about 2 weeks, just by introducing an occasional small amount of milk with their diet.

The cells sense the presence of a nutrient, and the enzymes are gradually induced until the intestine can then handle normal amounts. Bacterial infections and inflammation can cause the loss of lactase enzymes, and probably many other important digestive enzymes. And experiments with supplementing thyroid or progesterone have found that you can induce or restore the lactase that has been deficient just by increasing those anti-stress hormones." (Raymond Peat, Ph.D. Milk, Calcium and Hormones)

Cutting carbohydrates, cutting grains, cutting calories, cutting fat, cutting dairy, spending hours in the gym will not bring you closer to health or happiness. It's not about identifying your weaknesses and avoiding everything; it's about prompting and exciting your body to better adapt to become more efficient with the management of all the things we take in, ingest, and face in our modern life.

"If you went to a personal trainer and said, "My upper body is really strong, but the problem is my really weak, skinny legs," you'd probably find the trainer putting MORE emphasis on your weak spot and working the weak spot harder. Although this isn't an exact parallel to what you're about to experience, that ain't too far off." (Matt Stone. Diet Recovery)

I also heard from a nurse I met who grew up in the Philippines briefly, who heard my whole spiel about all the foods I was avoiding because I "reacted" to them and they were evil. He said, "Usually, when you are quote on quote "intolerant" to something, you just need to be exposed to it more, and we usually give the patient more of it, so they can build up a tolerance to it." Oh boy, did I feel the rage build up inside, because that is *not* what I or my restrictive DE mentality wanted to hear... But now, I can go back to that moment and give myself a little love tap to the noggin and soak that wisdom right in. It makes full sense now because that's what I did to handle foods again and reclaim my digestive health! That was one of those seeds planted in my dome, but just took a couple seasons to germinate.

When you cut out carbohydrates or fats, your ability to handle carbs when you reintroduce them goes way down. Glucose metabolism is altered and both your digestive and metabolic aptitude decreases. You can even raise your blood sugar levels to diabetic levels when reintroducing foods back in from the reduced ability to metabolize your glucose or other sugars. People then blame the fact that they get "foggy headed," gain weight after, get fatigued, are bloated and gassy, have cravings, break out, etc., on the fact that the carbohydrates have "proven" to be the enemy now. Therefore, they need to keep restricting their carbs or fats or whatever their case may be, which only continues the cycle. Do you know what a typical anorexic goes through in recovery? Their malnourishment and scarcity of nutrients and energy created many intolerances to most all foods and an inability to metabolize their sugars, which were problems otherwise absent before the dieting and eating disorder.

Excessive restricting, dieting, and/or anorexia results in your metabolism lowering, and the liver loses its ability to store carbohydrates in glycogen in the muscles. This can lead to bouts of hypoglycemia after or between meals, causing you to feel shakiness, irritability, anxious, etc. Ever since I personally began my first phase of my eating disorder as a teenager is when I felt hypoglycemic. After raising my metabolism in recovery, I no longer have these feelings if I eat balanced meals comprising fats, carbs, and proteins and eating enough. I can even go hours and hours without feeling shaky or crash now if need be. It's such a relief not to have to trip and stress about stuff like that now.

So, like I said, revamping your metabolism is not about continuing to fear the foods you cut out prior because you couldn't "tolerate" them before. It means gradually strengthening your digestive capabilities to digest and metabolize all foods again. This will broaden your dietary freedom from restrictions and limitations that are life sucking, draining, and unnecessary. We need to expand the foods you can "tolerate."

Same with now, after going gluten-free, dairy-free, soy-free, corn-free, grain-free, nut-free, or any of those elimination diets, people are now overly sensitive and have weakened their aptitude to handle these substances for when they try to add these foods back in and feel discomfort. They quickly determine that, yes, those foods were the culprit of all evil! So, they back themselves into a dark hole of fear, guilt, and restriction, and they don't truly ever feel better from the more restrictions they put on themselves. I know I didn't, and all the others I've spoken to and dealt with, so to get over this line, what you would do is slowly give yourself small amounts every day of the food, such as bread or milk or beans or whatever, and over time, you'll get over that sensitivity.

The more you cut out and restrict, the more sensitive and unable you are to handle the food when trying to reintroduce it, so let's think about these ENT (Ear, Nose, and Throat) doctors. They give you a long series of drops or shots to help you overcome your allergies, right? What's in that liquid? Tiny amounts of the substances, foods, pollens, pet saliva, you name it, that you are allergic to. "They contain a tiny amount of the specific substance or substances that trigger your allergic reactions. These are called allergens... This helps get your body used to the allergens (desensitization)." Over time, by giving your body gradually increased amounts of that allergen, your immune system becomes stronger and more familiar with that substance and your allergen to that diminishes.

When I first added back in ANYTHING other than fruits and veggies, boy did I feel it, and in many ways. Waking up with a swollen face and eyes, pains in my joints, shakiness, headaches, constipation, abdominal pains, painful edema, UTI's and so much more. Thankfully, after several months, I no longer had any of these reactions, and I felt in better health than I had in YEARS!!! I wanted to dance and do cartwheels every which way. I became that annoying child that bugs every tired and groggy dieting adult with my new burst of energy, laughter, and playfulness. But I'd take that over feeling sedated, weak, and malnourished, any day.

Plus, I did not have cravings anymore, since I wasn't restricting all these food staples my body needed. The elimination diets just send you to dietary prison, constantly trying to test what you can tolerate and what you cannot. You drive yourself crazy, because the more you eliminate, the more you react to those foods you seemed just fine with last month or even week! People end up not tolerating *any food* on these elimination diets, because they back themselves into corners, ruining their health, digestion, and metabolism by avoiding too many foods.

It's a tough pickle to be in... you react to every food, but the only way to get over that is to actually *eat* those foods. So, what do you do if you react to all these foods now?! Well, you have to *eat* still and push through the pains and discomfort, and *it just gets better*. Time and consistency heals. Remember, for the bazillionth time, the only way out is to eat! Try to add little amounts of the problematic foods every couple days, and slowly, over time, you'll be able to handle the foods again. I wish I had a better, more complicated, and rigid answer for your ED than that to digest, (no I don't ha!), but that's just what it takes. I was in this exact pickle, feeling I had no hope, and that my body was screwed, and there was no saving it.

Think of if you hadn't gone to the gym in a while or picked up running for the first time, and the first time back, you are SO SORE, or your heart is pounding, and you are out of breath, tire easily, and fatigue early on....this doesn't mean the exercise is *bad* for you; moving our bodies is one of the best things we can do for ourselves, but if you don't use it, you lose it, and this goes for digestion and elimination (the digestive tract is smooth *muscle*) from laxatives, enemas, not eating enough, or restricting types of foods, lowering your enzyme production, etc. It just takes time to work your body up to par, to better fitness, ability, and strength. You can't expect to have a day on the treadmill or one lift of a dumbbell and effortlessly and painlessly become Michael Phelps or Jackie Joyner-Kersee overnight.

Now, with all this being said on not being intolerant to some foods, there is a reality for certain people to be more sensitive to certain foods, and they would be better off avoiding those foods. Certain intolerances or sensitivities can lead to inflammation in the body, and if you know a certain food is the causative factor, truly and honestly, then please do not force yourself to push through the inflammation responses. But just because you react to a certain food does not mean it's reactive to everyone else and you should create a diet plan that's the new "cure-all" diet fad and preach it as if everyone should do it too.

Some foods that are inflammatory to others may not be inflammatory to another set of people. Just like how some people cannot tolerate onions but many people do, same goes for gluten. Some people truly have Celiac disease because they are part of the population that is more sensitive to gluten. This does not mean the whole population is sensitive to gluten and that everyone needs to go gluten free; many people go gluten free with no symptoms or reactions driving their decision. They just do it because they heard other people doing it and getting "results" (sometimes, they're really just telling themselves that to make it believable and doable; they try to convince themselves so they'll stick with it) and since it has become quite the fad diet change to implement. Some people can hold their alcohol well and never get ill, while others get deathly ill after one drink; some people get debilitated from MSG, where others have no pronounced reaction.

Don't talk yourself into being intolerant to something you're not, just because it's a trend to be intolerant to it. When I was growing up, the "cool kids" hated mustard, so the rest of the kids at school said how much they hated mustard, even though they clearly loved mustard before. The kids were made fun of and were told "eewww you're gross" if they got mustard on their food or admitted to liking mustard. So, they changed their beliefs just to *get along* and avoid conflict, sneaking in mustard at home, but still denying it to the kids at school. These days, it's dairy or gluten or corn or soy or eggs or meat or fruit... yeesh! Stop following what the "cool kids" are doing and be strong enough to stand in your truth and *do you*. Why are they so cool to you, anyway? They're just a human that requires oxygen, water, and fuel to survive like you; they may just have a nasty attitude and a more heightened ego. These bullies (and bullies come in all shapes, sizes, ages, genders, etc.) most likely have hidden insecurities that they project onto you to make you feel bad about yourself to make themselves feel better. I say, screw that.

FACING YOUR "FEAR FOODS"

I spent the first several weeks and couple months gorging on sushi, loads of bread, jars of peanut butter, sweet fruits like dates, ice cream, cereal, cheese, pizza's, Indian food lunch buffets, boxes of granola bars, and more, focusing way less on fruits and raw veggies.

If you need 2 weeks or 2 months straight of junk food to get over yourself and your self-proclaimed (or outside-sourced-"guru"-proclaimed) "fear of foods" and to get past the cravings, then do it! Seriously. Do. It. I think it's essential in the beginning of recovery. I needed it for months, and a lot of other people needed it as well. Eventually, if you allow yourself enough of the "forbidden" food, it will become just a normal food again, and your desire for it will become neutral. You most likely won't even want it anymore and may prefer more wholesome simple foods because of the way these foods make you feel.

If you keep labeling certain foods as either "bad" or "good" then you will continue to crave and binge on those foods. If you are craving a certain food, let's say, pizza, ice cream, chocolate, nut butter, etc., and you allow yourself to have it whenever you want and to your satisfaction, then the food will become less and less desirable. Also, the key is *not to feel guilt or shame after*, oh, and not restrict the next day "to make up for it" or "balance out good with the bad."

After you've been consistent with this, you won't feel the feeling of *losing control* if you have some of the food; you'll eat some and then move on without binging or thinking about it or dreaming about it. You'll go for another binge, and if you've been consistent with feeding yourself and not restricting, one of these times, you'll be shoveling the food into your mouth, and think "eh, this doesn't taste as good anymore." You won't be able to make yourself binge, even if you wanted to. Even if it's become a habit to binge, you'll just not even want to continue and be able to walk away.

Recovery is hard to attain, if not impossible, when you still hold onto fear foods and "good and bad" food lists. In recovery, you're not just working on your physical health, but also your mental health, and by allowing yourself to eat junky processed foods, it's very beneficial for your mental health's sake. You'll be able to create your own balance between wholesome foods and junk foods eventually; just do not eliminate or restrict junk foods, or you will crave them uncontrollably again. Do not have negative connotations for certain foods, whether it be "fattening foods" "bad foods" "addictive foods" "acidic foods." I mean people come up with many odd associations. I had laughable ones now, when I look back to my ED thoughts.

These fear foods promote ED behaviors, like obsessiveness and cravings. If one is trying to recover from anorexia or restrictive dieting, having a focus on "healthy clean foods" in recovery can be counterproductive for mental health, since eating disorders have a lot more to do with mental health than physical health sometimes. Research shows, just because you give yourself permission to eat junk food in recovery does not mean you are asking to form bad junk food habits. You're not going to become a junk food addict. Normally, recovered patients lean toward healthy food and lifestyle choices after treatment (such as focusing on health benefits of foods and avoiding trans fats (hydrogenated oils) and drive-thru fast food all day every day.

"When you avoid something that scares you, you tend to experience a sense of failure. Every time you avoid a

feared object or situation, your anxiety gains strength while you lose some. Every time you avoid the feared object or situation, you accumulate another experience of failure and another piece of evidence attesting to your weakness. Finally, avoidance eliminates practice. Without practice it is difficult to gain mastery. Without mastery, confidence is less likely to rise.

So, avoiding anxiety maintains and magnifies it. To get rid of your anxiety you should instead capitalize on the principle of habituation through the use of "exposure." Exposure is by far the most potent medicine known to psychology.

Exposure entails facing your fears, which makes it aversive in the short-term. But many worthy long-term goals entail short-term discomfort (think studying for an exam). Exposure also seems counter intuitive, but many truths are counter intuitive (think about the fact that we're residing on a ball floating in infinite space). Exposure scares people, but scary things are not necessarily dangerous (think roller coasters, horror films). Exposure is scary primarily because most people, lacking an understanding of the habituation principle, expect their fear to escalate indefinitely in the presence of a feared object or situation. But nothing rises indefinitely. And fear, if you face it, will soon begin to subside as you habituate. Thus with anxiety, the only way out is through.

Exposure isn't easy. However, living in the prison of avoidance isn't easy either, and it isn't much of a life. The short-term discomfort of exposure is the price we must pay to purchase a valuable long-term asset--a life free from debilitating anxiety." (Noam Shpancer PhD, psy-chologytoday.com)

Damn The Diets

Kartini is one of the only treatment centers for eating disorders that does not allow junk food (or high calorie, high
fat, or sweet desserts) while in treatment. How are people
supposed to break their mental ties to fear foods?! How do
psychologists break fears and phobias with their patients?
By having their patients directly face the fears/phobias, so
the client can face-to-face experience that exact scenario
they fear, with the result of showing them it will not kill
them or make them obese or whatever they may have
thought would happen. The more successful in the long
term seem to be the treatment centers that do not restrict
junk foods, but incorporate the challenging junk foods
along with the more healthier options.

It's in our nature that rules are meant to be broken; as
soon as you forbid or deem a food as off-limits, you will
want to break that rule so bad. That food will become your
kryptonite and your worst nightmare. It will be all you can
think of, dream of, or talk of. If you would just look at it as
what it is, simply an energy source, and have some when
you want it, it does not hold so much *power* over you.

Were you ever told as a kid by your parents or whoever,
"Don't stare at the sun for more than 8 seconds or else
you'll go blind!" How did you feel immediately after?!
Couldn't help your eyes from traveling right into the direct
view of the sunlight, trying to fight not to keep staring, but
it was so hard not to after you were told "no" (being told
not to stare into the sun is being told a form of *no*). When
you or someone says, don't do this or that, it becomes very
appealing suddenly, whereas before, it had no meaning or
draw to it, just prior. Please, kick the mental fear nonsense
to the curb. The fear and restriction is the devil on your
shoulder, whereas the acceptance and freedom is the angel
on your shoulder. Once you try to restrict certain foods,
you'll have intense hunger and cravings for those exact
foods in very large doses.

"How can eating disorder patients be expected to magically be okay with "normal" eating, particularly in social settings that will, inevitably, include cupcakes, chips, and soda, if they have not ever been exposed to such foods for an entire year in treatment? Treatments may benefit from focusing on reducing negative reactions to high-calorie foods through exposure therapy. Indeed, there was a large difference between implicit affect to high-calorie foods in the patient and recovered groups.

While Dr. O'Toole does not advocate for eliminating high-calorie foods—just so-called "junk foods," arguably, eliminating negative reactions toward all foods, including "hyperpalatable" or "junk" foods is also an equally worthwhile goal. Indeed, the cognitive behavioural model of eating disorders posits that binge eating occurs as a result of the inability to maintain rigid dietary rules. Consequently, eliminating the rigid and inflexible dietary rules should, in the long run, decrease binge eating—especially when the binge eating is triggered by a sense of failure to maintain the rigid rules (for example, eating a piece of a forbidden food leading to a sense of "failure" that precipitates a binge.)

AN-EXRP sessions emphasize the importance of intensifying and experiencing eating-related anxiety rather than avoiding it, and may involve maneuvers to highlight such anxiety (e.g., a session might incorporate holding a greasy food for a prolonged amount of time). These techniques allow the therapist (in collaboration with the patient) to enhance eating related anxiety and provide prolonged exposure to the situation such that the patient learns experientially that anxiety dissipates.

Personally, I believe that being encouraged, and at times, forced to eat chips and drink soda was an essential part *of my treatment. I also wholeheartedly believe that the danger of continuing to suffer from an eating disorder far outweighs the evils of processed food (no pun intended). If the choices are between severe restriction or frequent binge/purge episodes and Cheetos, I'll take the tasty little cheese bites any day." (*<u>scienceofeds.org</u>*)*

Challenge your dietary limitations. You won't ever get to dietary peace and namaste by avoiding foods you love and crave. Build that trust with your body again to let it know there is a surplus of everything it needs, fats, carbohydrates, protein, nutrients, and that if it is hungry, you will feed it. Once the body is comfortable and not stressed out thinking it will be put in a famine tomorrow or this afternoon, it can then shift into abundance mode and can burn energy to full capacity again. It no longer must slow down the metabolism to squeeze out every morsel of nutrition it can from the limited amount that's coming in and store that for later when it's not being fed sufficiently again. Most of our weight is regulated in the hypothalamus of the brain, and what is the hypothalamus's primary *preferred* fuel source? Glucose! Carbohydrates!

So, if you're a low carb-er, how is your hypothalamus supposed to function properly and regulate your weight when it's in a state of starvation? It's going to say CONSERVE!! STORE!! We are in a state of famine; we need to compensate for later!! Sh!% F@*$!!!!

Let me stop right there and add a mini-rant... this doesn't mean you need to be low-fat, high-carb, though. You just need to figure out a ratio of carbs that makes you feel *your* best; that may be a smaller portion of carbohydrates or a larger portion. Nope, I refuse to provide percentages for these portions. This may be because you may not need as many carbs as someone who is active, but you still need a good amount regardless. With that said, even some very active people claim to do better with higher fat than carbs (not higher like 70/30 just a smidge people! (I can already see you turning this into an obsessive habit). Anyway, therefore, they follow that way of eating because it better suits them, not because they're following a Ketogenic diet and they're forcing their body to eat virtually no carbohydrates.

Perhaps they may come from a European genetic background and are better adapted to a higher fat diet when comparing to an Asian background that has been better adapted to a higher carbohydrate diet. Yet still whether Asian or Europen, they all still include the basics of fats, carbs, and proteins, just in different ratios or proportions. Some people may hear this and think "oh yes, I'm European so I must be Ketogenic now." When really this is not what being from a European background entails. Get the point?

And by figuring out a ratio, I don't mean going on to chronometer and jumping on Instagram and following a bunch of #IIFYM (if it fits your macros) people. I mean spoon some carbs and fat (not with measuring tools) onto your plate and see how you *feel* with that amount. If you get full before you finish your plate or don't feel as well when you get to the end of the meal or just after finishing the meal, or if you're still hungry and wanting more, then proceed with either eating more or less. You also may do better with *different* carb sources (potato vs grain; white rice vs brown rice, etc.). Experiment! It's all trial and error. There's no failure in this except that you are not trying nor taking risks. That's failure to thrive as a free individual. Ask yourself, why is it, for those with Eating Disorders, so scary to try new things without a set of guidelines? *End Rant*

"But really the only way I recovered from my eating dis-order and chronic dieting was to never ever restrict. Nev-er restrict ANY kinds of foods, not even the portion sizes. And that really is the only way food loses its power over you. If you can have something every day as much as you want, you tend not to want it as much anymore. And af-ter a period of time, you actually eat what your body needs, you eat what makes you happy, and you will not think about food ever again! And that is how I healed my-self." (Portia de Rossi, on Oprah Winfrey Show.)

Once you overcome these dietary restrictions, and the in-ner filing system you've created for yourself of "good" or "bad" food lists, and you've reached a point where you aren't stressing about every morsel that's landed in your mouth, you can get to a point of *choice*. You can now choose to eat nutritious foods, for the sake of how you feel from certain foods, because you know they are nourishing for your body, and you do this because you love yourself and you're doing it for yourself, not for someone else's rules, guidelines, or theories. And when you don't eat a wholesome, home cooked, organic, grass fed, main ingre-dient=love, yada yada type meal, the junky food you eat instead will still also nourish you if your body is asking for it.

Yes it's nice to eat wholesome foods and home-cooked meals. And when I say whole foods, I'm not saying elimi-nate healthy oils (olive/ghee/butter/coconut) and that you must get your fats from the food itself, and I'm not saying eliminate breads or pastas because it's blended down to a flour, and I'm not saying don't eat salt unless it comes from the food itself, you get the idea? Rather, I mean try to aim for wholesome foods that are not artificially made in a lab. But if you need to, sometimes, for mental ease or crav-ings, then indulge! Do it!! Eat any foods you desire, as much as you care for, and do it *consistently*! This will elim-

117

inate all your urges to binge. It will eliminate cravings, and it will restore normal hunger cues. You'll start to crave more wholesome simple meals and the intense cravings for processed junk foods alleviates, and you are not all-consumed anymore.

If you have tried to be raw for any period of time (or have otherwise been on a very "clean and pure" diet) and then went back to eating cooked food or more processed foods, you can have a lot of digestive issues arise. You may feel like your body has become so pure it simply cannot digest those "toxic" foods anymore. Many raw foodists or "clean eaters" tend to yo-yo back and forth between 100% raw or 100% clean and to cooked food binges or junk food binges, only to return to more cleansing and detoxing and an even stricter raw food diet or stricter clean and pure diet. They find that, whenever they eat cooked food or processed food, it totally "destroys" them. A bowl of rice will make the raw foodist pass out, as if they ate a big Thanksgiving dinner, and eating out at the restaurant causes them to feel so sick they'll spend a week recovering from it.... same with the clean eater eating a meal with bread or cheese or anything somewhat more processed. Raw foodists and Clean Eaters incorrectly assume and believe their bodies have become so pure (as in "super healthy") it now rejects the toxic cooked foods or poisonous processed foods that most people are familiar and adapted to.

In reality, what's going on is the "raw food" body has simply stopped producing the right mix of digestive enzymes, so they simply can't properly digest more complex foods now. By eating only foods that require almost no digestion (like fruit), their digestion has "dumbed down" to the point where it can handle nothing more complex. Some raw foodists take this to even more of an extreme, making their diets even stricter with time, eliminating fatty foods like nuts and seeds entirely. This leads them to become even more sensitive.

The same phenomenon happens in reverse. Someone eating a pure junk food diet, devoid of fiber with lots of meat, white bread, and few to no vegetables, can experience some serious digestive discomfort when they eat lots of fiber-rich foods, like beans or fruits and vegetables. It can take them weeks or months to adapt to this new healthy diet.... The trick to avoid the "raw curse" is to retrain your body to digest certain foods. You can do it for almost anything. And eventually, eating a bowl of brown rice won't put you in a coma, and having a little garlic in your stir-fry won't cause you to have nightmares all night! (Raw Controversies, Frederic Patenaude)

This thing can happen with any food you have eliminated from your diet. It does not mean the reason you cannot digest the "toxic" foods anymore is that your previous diet was so "pure." I experienced this raw food curse often. Every time I eliminated foods from my diet, and the purer and cleaner I got with my eating, the fewer foods I could handle and digest. Every little thing seemed to cause trouble. But I thought if I continued to be strict and eat clean or raw like that, then soon, I could eat anything without problems. And I have seen so many people in the raw food movement experience the same thing. They have trouble digesting some foods most of us would consider healthy. Your body needs time to adapt to the foods previously eliminated.

Processed foods are not necessarily junk food. Processed foods are also things like yogurt, whole grain breakfast cereals or breads, canned beans, nut butters, and even frozen vegetables. The number one reason high-calorie processed foods are recommended in recovery is because they are pre-processed, making them easier for your body to digest and, therefore, easy to get energy from.

Don't fill yourself up with lots of low-calorie, water-rich fruits and veggies. This will only balloon you up, because you have to eat too much to feel satiated and get enough calories. Eat more high-carb foods (tubers, rice, potatoes) and add fats to make food calorie dense (oils, avocado, nuts, nut butters). If fiber bloats you, then choose regular pasta instead of whole wheat and white rice instead of brown rice – or just eat more processed foods in general.

You can do this vegetarian if meat absolutely disgusts you, and you've been vegetarian for most of your life, even as a kid. There's a difference, where you're just training your mind to be grossed out of meat because you've chosen to be vegan or vegetarian following a guru's or leader's sug-gestions. Personally, I am not a vegetarian and if my body's craving meat, or a loved one cooked something with meat, or I'm out at a restaurant, I'll eat meat. And yea, I try to get good humanely sourced meat when I can, but if I'm in a situation where I can't get it, I don't freak and stress out about it. I do my best for the situation I'm in. So, the moral of this story is, if you absolutely cannot do meat, you can do so and recover fully if you incorporate dairy prod-ucts. If you're vegan and not seeing the improvements you've been seeking, try to branch out and at least have eggs and dairy products in your diet as a substitute. If you're eating and can tolerate milk and dairy products, you don't have to eat meat.

I will say, to be vegan and fully recover, can be too risky for many people and too restrictive for recovery; I tried to continue with recovery staying vegan, and I followed sev-eral people who claimed to recover as a vegan, but in reali-ty, for a lot of them, it was just the ED mindset switching from one restrictive diet to another, which now they are eating *more* but still restricting important diet components that some animal products offer us and that we've adapted to require as a species over the past hundreds of thousands of years. Like I said, I tried recovering as a vegan for 6 more months (after being vegan for about 4 years), but still had some very pronounced symptoms that did not go away until I added in some animal products to my diet, such as cheese, milk products, and eggs and some meat weekly, such as chicken. Even eggs alone did not help rid these symptoms, but the milk products and some meats, did. Although eggs alone took away my GERD symptoms and acid reflux, if I felt symptoms of GERD or the like, and I ate eggs, the symptoms subsided almost immediately.

Some of the other symptoms I'm talking about were night tremors, limbs going numb, shaking, nose bleeds (which I never got nose bleeds in my life, even as a kid), and some other symptoms. I was also finally "satisfied" with my meals and quicker into the meal. I used to have to eat huge bowls or plates of food to feel satisfied. And I would get looks of "damn that's a big bowl of lots of food..." I did not care though, because I knew I needed it whether people understood why or not. I eventually could eat smaller bowls of food and be satisfied. But I had to go through the big bowl phase to get to the small bowl phase. And I still sometimes have waves of "I need a big damn bowl, right now."

A lot of us cannot undo our evolution and physiological adaptation for many generations all around our globe for our need to incorporate forms of animal products in our diet. Just because it recently made some sense theoretically to go animal-product-free, we cannot go back hundreds of thousands of years and think our body's going to go right back with us and be all hunky dory. It doesn't work like that, especially for those with European backgrounds like mentioned previously. If our body gets certain nutrients, already bioavailable, from an exogenous (outside) source, the body then stops the ability (over generations) to produce certain nutrients. Animal products are this, bioavailable forms of nutrients that the animal digested for us, and now our body can easily utilize. Plant sources are much harder for humans to digest and assimilate, which is why we started cooking our foods, to further assist the breakdown of cellulose amongst other vegetable matter, to more easily extract the nutrients. We produce no form of cellulase (the enzyme needed to break down cellulose), but it's interesting to note our bodies adapted in a way where we now produce carnosinase (an enzyme produced in the human digestive system and other human tissues, needed to digest carnosine — a protein found only in animal tissue — and some carnosine is absorbed in intact forms by intestinal cells) (Sadikali et al. 1975). We also adapted in a way where we produced amylase in our saliva, which is the enzyme needed to break down starch.

Same with egg cholesterol; this is *good* cholesterol that lowers *bad* cholesterol (LDL), but raises the *good* cholesterol (HDL). The good cholesterol is used for so many functions in the body, such as anti-inflammatory processes and to make up every cell membrane in the body. Cholesterol is also the main precursor to the formation of many of our hormones such as DHEA, testosterone, progesterone, pregnenelone, etc.

"Cholesterol is the raw material from which our bodies make all of the sex hormones such as estrogen, progesterone, testosterone and others. It is also the raw material from which we make all of our adrenal hormones such as adrenalin, cortisone, and aldosterone. Thus, cholesterol is not a bad substance, as some are made to believe by their poorly informed physicians.

Also, most cholesterol is made in our bodies. I have had vegetarian clients with elevated cholesterol levels who ate no animal products whatsoever. The only time cholesterol is a problem is when it is very high. This is a stress indicator, and a liver imbalance. Eating the correct food, which includes some high quality animal foods, can help lower a high cholesterol when that food is eaten properly in combination with other high-quality foods such as plenty of cooked vegetables, and when a person takes the correct nutritional supplements with it. In fact, healthful fats, including some cholesterol, at times, are critical nutrients. For much more about cholesterol, read Cholesterol-phobia on this website." (Dr Lawrence Wilson).

I could go on and on and try to convince you, but I'm not here to convince, just to share insight, so I'll leave the decision up to you. Because, honestly, if veganism works for you, then that's great. Keep going with what feels best for your body. Veganism does not work for everyone, but it can work for some if done strategically, and even then, it still can't work for some. My intentions for these explanations to support animal product consumption is for those that are so deeply engrained within the veganism mindset and dogma. Even though their health is going to shit right before their eyes, they continue to persist without animal products, and will give no consideration to change because they feel too ashamed or guilty or committed to their cause or community. I can understand this situation because I was there; I wanted veganism to work for me so badly that I wouldn't let go of the diet ideology, despite the obvious signs that my health was crumbling to pieces and I felt the worst I'd felt in my whole life.

Your health is just as important as the animals you're sacrificing for. We are all equally important. Your health as a human species here on earth has an equal priority with the animals to deserve health and freedom. And if your health is suffering after going vegan, it's time to swallow your pride, de-fog your dogma goggles, and be open to and okay with change. And if it's not, carry on!

Do you feel rage when someone questions your eating habits?

If at any point, you read through the suggestions and considerations to follow and behaviors you need to give up and you wanted to have a tantrum or immediately justified in your head "that you can still exercise, restrict certain foods, or do this by yourself and recover from your ED because somehow you are different," you need to get over yourself. Your ED is just trying to fight for survival; denial, manipulation, and justification are its best asset.

KNOWING TOO MUCH ABOUT "NUTRITION"

Try to, or better yet, make it a priority to throw out a lot of the nutritional conditioning you've learned. Try to relearn what makes sense and resonates to you and don't look back. Don't compare your decisions, after you've already followed your instincts, but feel guilty or 'wrong' compared to what Becky's doing. A problem for most of us is not to *learn* more, but to *unlearn* and deprogram a lot of the bullshit we've been told throughout our lives.

"Just ways in which you follow some strict and highly disordered form of eating until you: 1- Want to eat something else 2- Crave something else so badly you can't resist eating it 3- Develop health problems forcing you to eat something else. And when you do drop off the diet, you'll have a horrible time digesting and metabolizing the food or foods that you've omitted." Matt stone, Diet Recovery.

In the modern world nowadays, there are plenty of ways to mask your disordered eating to be societally acceptable from "being healthy" to "being spiritual" etc. Being vegan, and being a fitness model and competitor, personally, and for many recoveries out there I've worked with allowed us to showcase our eating disorder in public, and it allowed us to indulge in eating disorder behaviors without judgment but with praise.

No longer did we have to hide the Eating Disorder, but we could excuse our food restrictions nicely and rather eloquently behind a vegan shield or fitness shield. We could also kid ourselves that because of the fact that we were "eating healthy" or just "eating more again" and "exercising" that we were beating Anorexia or our other restrictive eating disorders of the past. When in reality, the Eating Disorder had just taken a different form.

No matter how fashionable and attractive food restriction and 'specialty restrictive diets' are in the modern world, we have to overcome this draw and temptation to brush over us, without us latching on and taking control. No matter how many friends are doing it, no matter how many sources tell us its healthy, no matter what, don't get suckered back into this nonsense and sad cycle.

Leave behind the quest of trying to seek the "perfect, most optimal, one-diet-for-all." The only perfect diet is the one you make for yourself based on the foods you love and make you feel your best. It's that simple. Just eat. Nothing is out of the question anymore. That's the beauty of recovery and normal living.

"I can still hear you going off on a tangent about the stuff you've read about fructose, the processing of table salt, the glutamic acid in soy sauce, the hormones in ice cream, the evil villainous gluten, the lack of vitamins or fiber in white flour, or otherwise. As someone who spent the better part of a decade wrapped up in such relative minutiae, I highly encourage
encourage you to let go of a lot of that fluff and give this a try.

Your fears and the things you are ideologically tethered to from excess internet health reading will hopefully fade pretty quickly until you are eating a more sustainable and socially-reasonable diet, and feeling a heck of a lot better than you were when intellectualizing every last detail of your food choices.

If you're not hip to that, that's fine too. As Uncle Rico said in Napolean Dynamite, "Stop wishing, and call me when you're ready."

The answers to better health, I have found, are mostly found in the simple realm. And there is no better guide to anything than our own tastes, appetites, and thirsts. Disobeying our body's cries for certain things, overriding our instincts, and exerting stubborn willpower is where we create the most damage, generally-speaking.

You'll really see why my work has taken me away from the small, trifling matters of nutrition and guided me to the bigger, more significant aspects of basic human physiology."
(Matt Stone, Diet Recovery)

We are a society obsessed with diets, weight loss, flat stomachs, and "clean eating." Every day, we are bombarded with images on social media (and other forms of mass media) about what the "ideal" body looks like. We have been conditioned to believe that being thin is more "desirable", and the simple way to achieve this is only through dieting. We live in a society that promotes being *fat* as bad and *eating* equals weakness.

Heck, as Matt Stone, a well-known metabolism expert, puts it, we're living under the guidelines of the "United States of Anorexia." This has created so much dysfunction and confusion for us; we are going against our physiological nature to achieve a false and unsustainable aesthetic ideal. There are no panaceas! There are no magic pills! There are no quick fixes! There is no diet that restricts something and is sustainable and healthy for the long term. The natural laws of nature just do not work like that. Anything worth having takes time, patience, persistency, and work. We need to stop comparing to others and create our own standard that allows us to be our best version of ourselves and allows for the best quality of life!

Every time you diet and restrict, you slow your metabolism and you teach your body to store fat. When you go off your diet, your body does not burn as many calories as it did prior and you'll put on even more weight than you had before. Your set-weight point will naturally climb higher and higher each time as you binge and store after each diet fails. Your metabolic fat burning mechanisms won't be able to function properly when starved. You cannot think about weight loss in recovery. That should be the least of your concern. It's time to reprioritize what's more important to you; focus on nourishing your body, healing your body, reestablishing trust with your body, and then balancing weight will come as a result later if it's supposed to. Do not restrict ever again!

"What you do on occasion is inconsequential, and living a good, fulfilling, and healthy life goes far beyond what a "perfect diet," whatever that is, can give you. A diet can really be so healthy it destroys your health, and more importantly, the overall quality of your life. You simply must stop attaching utopian happily-ever-after fantasies to various ways of eating. People will try to seduce you with all kinds of "sure things" against disease or weight "problems," but when you feel the urge to check them out, slap yourself in the face. If you have a longstanding dieting problem, you should probably never read another health or diet-related book again (except the ones that reinforce body acceptance, non-dieting, and other helpful things instead of distracting messages), just like someone with a heroin problem probably shouldn't shoot up again. You've already spent way too much of your mind energy

and time on intellectualizing and controlling everything you put in your mouth, and you've got a lot of missed life to catch up on." Matt Stone, Diet Recovery.

EATING RECOM-MENDATIONS... KIND OF..

The focus should be mainly shifting from restricting wholesome foods to eating whatever wholesome foods you desire, when you want, and to your satisfaction as the staple, and eat any junky fun foods you crave as more of a supplement.

It's okay and encouraged to want to be healthy and have a good, balanced diet and healthy exercise regime. However, the point you're trying to achieve here is to quit the obsessive thoughts and behaviors that dictate your life, so you can say *yes* more than no to opportunities and social gatherings around food and have fun in life or reclaim your life stolen from you from your restrictive disordered eating. You can also be able to say *no* to things you truly don't want to say yes to, because you are more in-tune with your intuition, and you are confident in what serves you and what does not.

Eat how you desire and when you desire. Some people do well having meals every 2-3 hours (like on the 7-day meal plan I offer) with 3 main meals and 2-3 snacks between. Others do better with 3 larger meals a day with no snacks, just following their hunger signals, eating when they're thinking about food, and eating until complete satiation, and stopping so they're not overstuffed sick.

I give the form of meal guides pertaining to eating smaller meals every 2-3 hours, because in the beginning of recovery, you're likely to be so out of touch with your inner hunger and satiety signals to guide you, you need to get a sense of how much you should eat, knowing it is okay and necessary to eat that much food and that often. When in a restricted and malnourished state for so long, the illness blocks your abilities to feel hunger, which feeds the cycle of not eating and restricting. You will get your hunger back as you go along; trust me. For now, or for the first couple months of recovery, you just have to eat, regardless of *feeling* hungry, to gain weight.

When starting recovery, the amounts you eat, you may feel you must be shameful for it or still feel like you're eating a lot, when really, you're not eating *nearly* enough.

Don't make yourself sick by overeating, but make it a habit to eat until satisfaction. Rewire your brain to know that eating to satisfaction and fullness is OKAY; restricting yourself from eating when you're still hungry after your dainty meal is *not* okay! Those hunger signals are there for a reason! Your body does not lie to you. Your body is not there to "make your life harder." Your body is not making you hungry to *resist* it. Your body doesn't overthink food like your conditioned, brainwashed diet-mentality *mind* does. You're doing your body a huge disfavor by ignoring and suppressing its cry for fuel. Don't leave your plate when your stomach is only 80% full and you're still wanting food. Leave when it's 100% *satisfied,* not stuffed and uncomfortable.

If you have been consuming under 1,000 calories a day for more than a week, if you've been abusing laxatives, enemas, diuretics, if you have a history of purging, or are coming from a fruitarian/raw vegan diet, you must increase your intake of foods slowly until you get your calories up to at least a minimum of 2,500 calories.

Like I'll mention again, digestive enzymes will help alleviate some nausea and digestive discomfort initially (perhaps not all). Anything helps though, right? So, try to increase your calorie intake every 2-3 days by 200 calories and more dense foods. If you feel fine and have a strong urge for food without ill symptoms, then you don't have to go this slowly. After you get to 2,500 calories a day and are feeling good, go straight in to 3,500+ calories a day, every day.

I'm confident your appetite will come back by this point and will come back with vengeance, as if a beast has awoken from the dead and wants to eat everything in sight and never wants to stop.

Insufficient calorie intake and restrictive dieting are directly linked to emotional ups and downs, body pains, blood sugar imbalances, digestive issues, fatigue, loss of hair, cravings, imbalanced hormones and many more. You'd be surprised to find out that a lot of your cravings for junk food, refined sugary foods, etc. are almost diminished once you fill your body with healthful and wholesome foods, such as quality dairy fats, quality meat, local organic fruit, vegetables, tubers, lefumes (not a typo) (peas, lentils, beans), whole grains (or white-washed grains), such as rice, oats, etc., and the *key* is to eat all these foods to your satisfaction and NOT cutting yourself short.

This is how I could finally focus on other things in my life again! This is how I set my mind free. I no longer was scavenging for any piece of junk food in the house and then binging out eating pounds of the food, but instead was actually quite *sickened* by the thought of eating it, because I was just not hungry for anything else, resulting in me forgetting about it, or just *easily saying no* to anyone's offering. A jar of chocolates or a bag of my favorite chips could easily sit in the pantry in my direct vision every time

Damn The Diets

I walked by, and it would not even phase me, call my name, or tempt me. Can you imagine that? That's freedom and true positive *control* right there!

Take advantage of this time, after dieting for years and years; you may eat whatever you want and a lot of it! Enjoy this time and savor every bite; it's such a pleasurable and freeing experience; it's something refreshing to embrace.

Don't take my plan as a finite, but as a guide to help support your desire and need to eat. I didn't eat all these foods initially. My diet and what I was eating was all over the place. I'd wake up in the morning and have a massive feast of several bowls of oatmeal, drenched in maple syrup or honey, a couple bowls of puffins cereal or granola and milk, a half a loaf of bread with jam and butter, half a jar of peanut butter with different fruits, such as tons of apple bananas (Hawaiian variety), papaya, pineapple, dates, etc. (yes, that was all in the same meal, crazy to think all that can fit in the stomach and still be wanting, eh?). Then at lunch, which was often only a couple hours after that, I'd go to sushi and get about 10 rolls or maybe get a burrito and endless chips and salsa. Then (yep, same meal), I'd have another half a jar of peanut/almond butter with 10 apple bananas, and at night, I had a couple cans of refried beans with cheese and then several bowls of granola with milk, or spaghetti, sauce, and parmesan, and THEN sometimes, I'd wake up in the middle of the night SO hungry and eat something else! Yea, I went hard once I passed the initial breakthrough of absent hunger and realization I needed to recover. I didn't cook many home cooked meals, because at this point, I was in Hawaii still, with no access to a full kitchen. Even in the house I ended up renting from, I didn't want to cook a dinner the size of an army and them see me eating all of that; yea, I was still lacking confidence with the situation I was in (but honestly who freakin cares! Screw 'em if they say something!).

Did I mention I was vegan for almost 4 years? Well, if you are a vegan, ketogenic, Atkins follower, (or whatever other restrictive diet philosophy) please reconsider this decision of yours. For anyone coming off any restrictive diets and eating disorders (yes, they're all classified together, diet trends, anorexia, over exercising fitness competitors, raw vegans, Ketogenic. You all have an eating disorder), you need to have the fewest restrictions and the most nutrition flooding your body at this time.

For veganism and macrobiotic, the nutrients found in dairy products and even quality meats, if you crave meat (this pertains to vegans), are very important and nourishing for you. It's fair to say dairy's a complete macronutrient; it is replete of carbs, proteins, fats. It's very balanced for regulating blood sugar and lowering inflammation. It also contains a lot of pro-thyroid and progesterone properties at the same time, which are anti-inflammatory in nature, where estrogen is more inflammatory in nature. Don't even come at me with the "Oh, it's mucus forming! Oh, but it's inflammatory, oh, but we're the only species that drinks another species' milk!" I don't want to go into detail in this book; I can leave the boring studies and statistical research for another day, book, blog, whatever.

For Paleo, dairy, beans/legumes, and grains, such as oats, rice, and yes, even wheat for some, have many health benefits nutritionally and health in means of your colon, amongst others. And eating as many nuts and meat as they do daily is not so pleasant for everyone, including many former paleo superstars, emphasis on *former*.

These have all been included in tribes and cultures all around the world free from illnesses and diseases for hundreds of thousands of years. This does not apply to the cultures that have since then adopted more western type diets and lifestyles, which then saw the rise in diseases, such as heart disease, obesity, diabetes, etc. The thing about tribes eating meat is that they didn't always consume meat 3 times a day, like you see nowadays. If we're not including tribes, such as the eskimos and alike, most tribes ate meat maybe once a day, a few times a week, or even just a couple times a month; the meat was not processed either. They also appreciated, respected, and humanely sourced and consumed the meat. These tribes showed no signs of degenerative diseases. But today, meat eating is a whole different ballgame. Decide for yourself for what you want to do.

The statement that claims vegan or 100% plant based diets with zero animal products have all the nutrients we could ever possibly need is a flawed and untrue statement; for many people who go vegan, they watch their health decline dramatically and quickly. It's important to have a good amount of your diet from plant foods, but not always 100%.

We still, in human nutrition, don't have a full grasp on every nutrient and micronutrient and all the other many components that go into nutrition for the human body. We are just now getting into the technology we need to understand nutrition science. You understand this in biochemistry and classes of the like. Nutrition science is a young science and we have not had the technology and the methods nor the capacity to research it and really know everything about it. For example, in 2003, a study came out with the findings of a new and unknown vitamin (some people argue it's a cofactor), a nutrient humans need, and we are just finding out about it, after so many diets have run their course.

In plain, we just don't know what nutrients humans require; it's an unknown variable. The only way to make sure you will not fall into nutritional gaps is not to restrict food groups. There may be a nutrient we don't know about that's in our traditional foods we've been eating for hundreds of thousands of years, for example, a nutrient in red meats or milk products not found in eggs or plants.

Some people with older genetics, from when we migrated and adapted long ago, when we were more plant based as a species compared to the modern-day human, can biochemically take substrates and manufacture that nutrient for their bodies. Unfortunately, many people, through genetic variation, have lost those capabilities to do so.

A lot of vegans know and openly admit their health could be better if they included animal products in their diet, but refuse to because of their morals and ethics; they are willingly sacrificing their health and wellbeing for the cause. This can be avoided, if you simply put your money towards humanely sourced animal products. I'll leave the discussion at that, before I get crucified by the vegan community. I've already risked this often speaking out on Facebook, oops! And I get it. I used to be a die hard vegan myself, and if anyone challenged my beliefs, I would get infuriated. Remember to keep an open mind. It saved me.

The most "pure" and organic diet on earth means nothing if your body is not functioning properly. You need to get your body healthy and fix your relationship with food again before you can even think about looking into nutritional advice again, but I strongly urge you not to go down that road again, unless it's books about nutritional freedom and body acceptance!

Any diet restrictions can get turned into obsessions, even within veganism and paleo, especially for people with a past and current persona that takes things to the extreme and has disordered eating habits. I understand the ethical standpoints of vegans; I mean, seriously, don't hate on me for promoting animal products. I was a vegan for years, and vegetarian on and off for a lot of my life. I respect vegans and still like to get animal products from sustainable and humanely raised sources. That's what veganism is mainly about, anyway, the stance against inhumane living conditions and slaughter of animals these days. Despite the best of moral and health intentions of veganism, the vegan diet does not allow most humans to thrive.

Okay, so I'll get back on topic now. If you need something to go by, here's my nutritional advice, and all you really need.... First, eat a balance that's high in everything and not low- anything or any percentages. Try to stick to wholesome foods as the staple, whole grains (or even white rice is great, and I know of the controversy on this one), fresh humanely raised meat, dairy, and egg products, fruits, vegetables, legumes, nut, seeds, and quality oils, such as coconut, olive, ghee, butter.

Second, DO NOT stress or restrict yourself from indulgences and cravings; as a supplement to your diet, if you want cookies, ice cream, burgers and fries, or whatever else that suits your fancy, eat it, and savor every bit without guilt, shame, anxiety, or stress. Eat all your meals until you are satisfied and no less. Eat a balance of fats, carbs, and proteins at every meal in the ratio that makes you truly feel your best. No more foods or meals that are low-anything (low- sugar, carb, fat, salt, protein). Eating fat does not make you fat. Don't fear fat. Fat is the most critical hormone-producing outlet. Honor your cravings; honor your body's gift of communicating with you what it needs and when which makes it simple for you if you just tuned in!

Make full fat dairy (or even goat and sheep dairy) products and/or quality meat sources a priority to add into your diet. Try to think of yourself as a newborn baby... you need the extra easily-assimilated nutrients, and lots of them, to rebuild your body, as quickly as you can, as you did with mother's milk. But now, you'll be doing it with cow, sheep, goats milk, butter, yogurt, cheese, or egg products. And don't stop consuming them after you're recovered! The other priority to add into your diet is a complex carbohydrate starch source, such as white/brown rice, potato, sweet potato, wheat, oats, bread, pasta, etc., whatever starch source your body craves and does well with and you love. These two things will be the saving grace of your recovery along with the balance of everything else and for your health maintenance from here on out.

That's it. That's all the dietary advice you need. The rest is up to your body, so tune in and listen closely!

No more cleanses, no more detox's, no more restricting, no more counting calories, no more excluding whole food groups. No more fear foods, and no more "bad" cravings. Oh, and stop checking the clock to eat. Your body will tell you when it's hungry; if it's a designated time to eat and you're not hungry, don't eat. The same goes for if it's an hour after you just ate and you're hungry again, eat! If it's not noon, or it's after 6pm, but you're hungry for lunch or dinner, well simple, EAT! Your body knows better than you do. There's so much our bodies do for us every moment we don't even realize and take for granted, so if you're body's asking for fuel, you dang well better feed it. Because it most likely needs the fuel and nutrients for something we'll never know about or understand directly.

Let's talk about water drinking. I've heard both sides of the spectrum. Drink tons of water!! And drink no water!!! Well, I say, do what makes you feel best and follow your thirst signals. If you're not doing well or feeling uncomfortable from drinking tons of water, cut back. But if you try to drink less water and don't like the outcome, then drink more. In the beginning of recovery, you may experience edema or trouble metabolizing water and fluids, so it's been reported to cut back on water drinking. Another example is those fruitarians and raw vegans who say water drinking is "unnatural" and you must only get your water from the "a naturally filtered and distilled water" from your water rich raw foods. Yet another example is within the fitness world of dieting and cutting for fitness competitions or modeling photoshoots, where dehydrating the body by not drinking so much water and using diuretics to look leaner, tighter, more striated, and what not. I listened to all this advice, cutting my water intake dramatically and not listening to my thirst urges, but soon became constipated, lethargic, irritable, and noticed my energy drop amongst other things.

So, although I had edema during my recovery and was eating all raw foods during my Orthorexia days, my body still wanted more fluids, just not a whole gallon a day. I was chronically dehydrated, for many reasons, from my past disordered eating phases, so this was a healing method and way my body compensated for the lack of water for so long. Edema also helps speed up recovery, as it sets up for a slippery medium to transport nutrients to the damaged and depleted cells and tissues more rapidly and efficiently. I tried not to focus on the edema and kept drinking to what I felt was most optimum for me according to my thirst.

According to Traditional Chinese Medicine (TCM), a suggestion is to conserve your Qi; drink only when you're thirsty! Drinking eight glasses of water a day is not essential for your body's health and to stay hydrated or flush out the body's wastes. It's not necessary or healthy to use up your Kidney and Bladder Qi (the life energy that flows within us) like this. It also has the skill to maintain a healthy fluid and electrolyte balance. Trust your body's wisdom. It knows when you should drink. Listen to your body and not just your mind.

Coffee...People love their coffee... and I'm definitely not going to be the one to tell you to stop. If you want to drink coffee, fine, but perhaps, try to limit your intake to 1-2 cups a day, and load the coffee with honey/maple syrup/molasses and organic half and half; please no zero calorie or artificial sweeteners or stevia. If your intensions are to drink coffee simply for the appetite suppressing side effects, then you need not drink it, or you are feeding your ED, that simple. If you drink coffee to get up to go to work or school/studying, or just enjoy the taste, or the increased motility of the intestinal tract, then that's fine.

If people can sit there and promote coffee enemas up their butt, I can accept ingesting a cup of coffee in the morning via the mouth. And don't tell me it's different. I've tried coffee enemas, and I got just as jittery as if I drank it, and no, I didn't do it wrong or didn't have the wrong *kind* of coffee...like I mentioned before, someone as perfectionistic as me does not let anything wrong happen when embarking on something new; I go all or nothing, baby. Living in Hawaii changed my perspective on coffee, after cutting it out for several years. Let me tell ya, the nicest, most healthy, kind, smart, thoughtful, loving, supportive, non-judgmental and generous people I've ever met in Hawaii on the Big Island smoked a lot of marijuana and drank a ton of coffee (mmm Kona Coffee). If you want to have your dose of coffee, go for it. Another note worth mentioning is trying Yerba Mate Tea or Chai Tea with the half and half and molasses as a caffeine substitute or to cycle on and off with.

Let's also talk about salt intake. Salt is not this horrible entity that is out to destroy your health. In recovery, it's also imperative to make sure you're not cutting out the salt in your diet. Salt helps to raise and stimulate the metabolism and helps to support your adrenal glands. Salt with every meal (not to go overboard with the salt, but just enough) will help with digestion and raising your metabolic rate. I noticed I got very sweaty and hot after adding salt to meals initially. This is good; this means your metabolism is rising! I wasn't that sweaty forever though; it would just pleasantly warm me up, instead of being a walking ice cube unable to get warm.

OTHER THOUGHTS ON EATING...

So, isn't this whole thing about trusting your body, "eating intuitively," and listening to your cravings? Well, here's the thing...

At first, you may be at the point where you still will not realize how much quantity of food is necessary to eat. You'll still want to restrict your portion sizes or food sources. Its hard as shit to break these pointless loops telling us we need to restrict and avoid certain foods. That's the downfall, but also the goal of brainwashing!

What you need to know is, whatever you think is a "good portion" now, you need to triple that serving. At first, the stomach might reject foods altogether (especially for those fruitarians, raw foodists, and anorexics/extremely calorie restricted), and you will feel nauseous or even throw up. This is only in the very beginning of reintroducing foods, and what I found to help alleviate this was to take those digestive enzymes I mentioned earlier. I too felt very ill, even just eating fatty fruit, such as avocado and durian, or sweet potatoes, oils, and even cooked vegetables. Yes, steamed veggies after being raw vegan for so long made me deathly ill!

I used a brand, called MRM, named Digest All. I also used HCL and took twice the dose of these enzymes with every meal. This was a godsend since my digestion was so shot. I felt so ill with every food other than fruit and raw veggies. I only had to use these for the first month or two, which allowed me to get in a lot of energy and nutrients to strengthen and revamp my digestion and metabolism enough, so it could produce its own enzymes again and digest foods on its own again. I got a lot of aches and pains throughout my digestive organs in the beginning of recovery, painful I tell ya! But I kept pushing and persisting, because I knew I needed this, and after I got over the hump, the aches and pains became less and less often, and then were eventually nonexistent.

The human body *hates* irregularity; the body *thrives* on consistency. This means, your body will thrive on being constantly fed, whereas your body will go into starvation, hoard, and store fat for the famine mode, with inconsistency in eating times. This is because it does not know if or when it will get more fuel and nutrition, so starving it one minute, and gorging/binging the next.

I recommend ordering take-out or eating at restaurants or grocery stores or having a loved one prepare your meals for you. The reason for getting food from the restaurant or someone else's preparation not including you is because of several things: 1- It takes away your control and stress over making the foods yourself, stressing and obsessing about every ingredient you put into the food. 2- It takes the stress off cooking and it includes necessary ingredients you would have otherwise left out. 3- It's a good size meal (if you ordered an entree not just an appetizer) and you should eat the whole thing. Also, do not ask for "no-this or that"; take it or leave it the way it comes, unless you are *adding* something. I recommend take out, because perhaps, you're not ready to eat in public yet and want to do so in the comfort of your own home, which is understandable, but you better eat the dang food, and then some — yes, I mean, eat more than the entrée. You need more calories than a normal human that doesn't have a past of disordered eating and needs to recover from an ED. Remember not to skip any meals. Make it a priority. Remember,

Damn The Diets

your recovery is a priority right now. You are a priority. No exceptions.

For holidays and vacations, this can be stressful for most in the beginning of recovery; you will feel very uncomfortable, out of control, and anxious. This is a good test for you I feel, but can also be triggering if it truly is too stressful for you. If stressful, you know you have some serious work to do. You'll eventually get to where it won't stress you out anymore, and you'll be able to have a great time with loved ones and be able to do so without your thoughts being consumed around the food. It's good to be open with your family and close friends about what you are going through, just so they can be more understanding and supportive, and communication with anything is the key to success. It takes a great deal of courage to swallow your ego driven pride and show you're vulnerable and show you are struggling. It shows great character to admit you were wrong about your prior behaviors, and that you're trying to work on change. But in the act of this communication comes growth and strength. You got this!

The first Thanksgiving dinner I faced, about 11 months into recovery, was the first time I didn't stuff myself to the point of feeling sick, simply because I didn't want to... this is unheard of for me. Every year, I'd write in my diary as a reminder 'never ever again eat so much on thanksgiving or any holiday' because I always ended up in so much pain and agony from over stuffing myself. That holiday, I ate from every dish I wanted with no restriction and no second guessing. I felt no guilt after and no desire to keep eating and eating, and could stop when I was full, because I had no desire at all to keep eating, mentally or physically. I had a pleasurable time with my family and was not consumed with thoughts of food, but could have the brain space to focus on the true meaning of thanksgiving, spending time with loved ones.

144

No one truly understands what it's like to recover from an eating disorder or understand the disordered eating unless they've gone through it, worked with someone else with disordered eating habits, or done the research and educated themselves on what is involved, mentally and physically, and what to expect in recovery. My point is, if you're having trouble communicating to your family and friends, but they or you want them to understand, you can always send information to them so they can read all about it; this helps them gain a better understanding and grasp what's going on with you and why. With this knowledge they can be a better support outlet. You can let them read this book, or send them some other similar books, research, blog posts, or videos you've found elsewhere that explain the process. Luckily, my family was supportive of my recovery, whether they fully understood it or not, which I am forever grateful for.

WHAT TO EXPECT IN RECOVERY

The length of your recovery depends on the severity of your disordered eating. It also depends on how many relapses you have whilst in recovery and if you need to practice trial and error to find what works for you best. Mental recovery may take longer than the actual physical recovery, but it also might be the other way around; again, every recovery may look different for each individual. Usually, after the first 6-8 months is when your appetite calms down and you can eat "normally" and "intuitively" again, but don't be alarmed if the extreme hunger continues for you or comes in waves at a year or two in.

Do not panic if something you are facing is not mentioned. The list is long, and unique symptoms may happen to you that do not always happen for others. This is another point showing how each situation is entirely unique and based upon your body and many other factors. You must not look at everything mentioned as an absolute or an exact order or as an exact recipe to follow for success. Think of what you read and learn as an individual and varied recipe, mended to fit your unique needs. You may go into full recovery in 6 months, or you may take up to 24 months. Like I said, it depends on how long you were starved, environmental factors, if you stick to recovery to a T (more or less relapses), and many other factors. Just to note, 3 months is very rare for recovery, and 18 months is the average time for full recovery. That's a reminder, once again, to be patient; if you're not a patient person, then consider this time to be your learning lesson to develop patience. Use your time wisely.

Celebrate any and every small success along your journey and focus on the progress, rather than what you do not like about recovery. Remember to go easy on yourself and your body and give yourself a break. Your deepest and biggest fears may arise in recovery, and you may be forced to face them finally. You will probably face emotional and negative thoughts and feelings about how you feel about your body. You will have an ED battle inside your head about the good and the bad of what's happening.

You may have doubt about the process, and a voice will try to convince you you'll be much happier and it'll be easier if you just go back to restricting. You'll have many thoughts and presentations in your head trying to justify the disordered eating behavior. Don't cave; don't listen. Let the emotions and justifications flow, no matter how upset they make you, whether you have to cry for an hour or all day or for weeks straight to let it all flow out. Just don't let yourself be convinced to relapse or quit. The fears and thoughts are a normal and unfortunate part of recovery, but remember, they are what got you into this hellhole in the first place. They are not *you*; they are not *your* thoughts; they are your learned eating disorder trying to convince you to crawl back into the shithole and into restricting or over exercising or purging or whatever.

You cannot see relapses as personal failures, but instead, just accept them as part of the process, and each relapse will make you stronger for the next progress you'll be making. You need to give yourself time for self-reflection, to see how much progress you've made, and applaud yourself for even starting and sticking to it for a day, week, month, year, years, etc. Don't be too hard on yourself; it's not time to be a perfectionist. Once you finally learn from the mistake you keep making, you can finally move on; so, if you keep doing the same thing or making the same "mistake," step back and look at all the variables why you may need to learn a certain lesson from that mistake; what's the message that's trying to get through to you? Mistakes are just lessons in disguise, so we can learn and grow!

BINGING AND EX-TREME HUNGER

Restrictive eating has been scientifically proven to lead in-definitely to binge eating, extreme hunger, and long-term weight gain that is much harder to work off. Were you re-stricting your calories and food types for so long that, when you finally had an instance where you ate a "bad food", you went on a week, month, or several month-long binge that was uncontrollable? Were you into bodybuild-ing or bikini competitions that led to body dysmorphia and/or developed "binge eating" after? Were you down to a short list of foods you were allowed to eat being or-thorexic, that when you finally ate some cooked or junky food, you felt uncontrollable around the so called "addict-ing" cooked or processed foods? Or were you the average dieter who was trying to find the perfect diet so you could get the "perfect" body (according to society's standards), and you were told to restrict calories or certain foods, which inevitably led to binging when you couldn't stay on top of the restrictions?

Do not feel guilty if you eat 6,000 to 10,000+ calories in a day. Really. It's normal if you are recovering and severely malnourished from your restrictions and eating disorder. And if you eat this much one day, DO NOT restrict the next day to make up for it, no ifs, ands or butts! Remember, in the Minnesota Starvation Experiment, the men were some days eating 11,500 calories a day!

Restricted eaters most often are so out of touch with their hunger and satiety gauge that gives that sense of satiety after a meal, which leads to overeating. If this person would have never started restricting in the first place and never lost this intuitive guide, they would have known when to stop eating when the signals of true satiation arose. This could be explained as the feeling of "my stomach feels like a bottomless pit" or "my stomach is like a Marry Poppins bag." This most often happens to the restrictive dieter. You have not become a glutton, and you have not developed full blown binge eating disorder.

Binge eating disorder is on the opposite spectrum of restrictive eating disorders. Having a restrictive eating disorder, your system responds to leptin in your body correctly. Leptin runs your metabolism and appetite, once you are back to your natural weight set-point and not in starvation mode anymore; once your leptin levels get back to optimal levels, you will stop gaining weight. Leptin resistance is a hormonal state that causes your body to think it's starving and there's a scarcity in food. This keeps your metabolism lowered; therefore, your body continues to feel the need to store fat, even if you already have enough fat storage.

You'll maintain your weight naturally and eat when your hunger cues are there, when you get to your set weight point. It is not biologically possible for you to develop binge eating disorder and become obese; your body is just doing what needs to be done from being starved. Restore your weight and show your body it will be consistently fed, and your leptin response will work the way it is supposed to again. Listen to your hunger cues as much as you can; feed your body as much as you can as you listen to your extreme hunger. Your body desperately needs a lot of energy right now. Remember, every time you eat a lot or more than you think is "normal" in recovery, bingeing is not binging for you!

As one eats consistently, the more recognizable the satiety signal becomes as the body need not take in as many calories at every meal. Your body changes it's fear from assuming the next meal will not be satisfactory, and instead, you'll only provide it with limited and restricted fuel. It will now know and trust the next meal will be sufficient and you will give it what and how much it needs without restrictions. Many that experience binging during recovery then fear eating itself, because of fear of binging. What a mess.

"While dieters can consciously override the basic drive to eat for short periods of time, most cannot continue to do so. Hormones such as leptin and ghrelin that stimulate appetite after weight loss do not adapt quickly to reduced body weight. They continue to send out "eat more" signals for as much as a year after weight loss. Eventually, biology wins out." (Priya Sumithran, The New England Journal of Medicine)

Can't you understand yet why you're binging?! It's not something to be ashamed of and stopped! When you binge, do not purge in any form: throwing up, over exercising, or restricting. If you overeat one day, do not restrict the next day. Please and thank you!

There comes a point after consistently nourishing your body where you no longer have ravenous hunger. It settles down, and if you eat beyond satiety, you feel sick and literally grossed out by food. You'll also be able to stop after a "normal" meal as the average non-dieter person does and feel absolutely no desire for any food after or between meals. I bet you're thinking "um, yea right, that'll never happen for ME!" It will. Don't worry. If someone had told me this back when I was going through my extreme hunger and re-feed phase, I would've been like a deer in headlights, so confused and skeptical, and not able to grasp or even comprehend that thought. It had been so long in my life, that I was so confused with food, hunger, and normalcy, that the idea was so far-fetched; I couldn't imagine it could ever become *my* reality again. I thought I was too far gone, or that my situation and system was different.

It may be crazy to fathom a life of eating to satisfaction, and not limiting your portion sizes, and to listen to your bodily cues. It's more accepted and encouraged to inflict pain on ourselves in a more passive way, by restricting, and that's somehow more sensible and applauded by society, rather than listening to your intuition and bodies communication techniques. But truly, what needs to be done is trust your instincts and bodily cravings and EAT until satisfaction, and even past it in the beginning if need be, to get to sufficient calorie intake for successful healing and recovery.

You won't stuff yourself forever. The hunger obsession dies down and becomes more of what it is, just eating. You won't blow up to 300 lbs. It's hard to imagine this state of "normal eating" but you'll get there. If you truly want this and want to be free from this disordered eating, you will do what it takes, but you must take responsibility and face these restrictive demons.

WEIGHT RESTORA-TION

Weight restoration and maintained weight gain is *critical* and most important for recovery. When we are underweight and malnourished, our brain cannot function properly. We are not capable of thinking straight or thinking past our current beliefs and health dogmas. It's hard for our brain to make judgments and decisions effectively. With weight restoration, you can reclaim your brain as it's finally being fed and coming back to life. You are getting your brain and body to a point where you can trust yourself again to make mindful and rational decisions. You can create an environment and positive set of behaviors that your amygdala (grey matter inside each cerebral hemisphere, involved with the experiencing of emotions) no longer sees any food as a threat. It becomes easier to stick with recovery now that the unclouded thinking can be more effective and rational.

Weight restoration is also crucial for the rebalancing of hormones and females getting their period back. You might even need to gain a little over average and maintain that weight for months, and if this is so for you (as it was for me) don't freak out and start restricting again. That is exactly what your body needs; accept it for what it is and try to not focus on it. *Now* is the perfect time to work on self-acceptance, self-love, and healthy body image as mentioned previously.

Your **set weight point** is the point at which your body feels most comfortable, healthy, and stable. It does not matter what you eat that day, whether too much or too little; your body will stay within this range. And with range, I mean within several pounds. You will fluctuate; it is not an exact number 155, but more like 155-162. A set weight point is unique to everybody and is only determined by the body, as I mentioned before. Some bodies are curvier; some are skinnier. We are not and cannot be all the same size, shape, and weight. You can try to force your body to be a certain way, but it will be unhealthy, and you won't be able to sustain it. The media wants us to believe we should all be a certain BMI, and if not, we are unhealthy, fat, or anorexic.

This is not just for restrictive habits; even naturally skinny people must force-feed themselves to gain weight if they wanted to, and it would be very unpleasant. To maintain the weight gain, they would have to continue over feeding themselves to the point of sickness, and when they stopped this behavior, they would easily lose the weight and go back to their set-weight point.

This set weight point is inspired by hunger signals, satiety signals, and activity signals. This is a weight that your body functions best at and is in accordance to your genetic makeup. Your body will do anything to maintain its desired set weight point, no matter what you're trying to do externally. This is why, no matter how much you diet, cleanse, fast, and restrict, you may lose weight initially, but once you go off that diet, pill, cleanse, etc., your body will bounce right back to this range. You cannot control this for long. Remember, biology will win this game.

"Our set-point is determined by a series of hormonal signals released from our gut, pancreas, and fat cells, which travel to the hypothalamus in the brain. The brain then regulates how much we eat, how many calories we burn, and how much body fat we store long term through various hormones and neurotransmitters, such as serotonin, leptin, and ghrelin. Our "set-point weight" refers to the

level of stored fat our body automatically works to maintain regardless of a number of calories we take in or burn off. Our set-point explains why it's so hard to keep fat off through traditional diet and exercise techniques." (Bailor, A Calorie Myth.)

During a year, maybe two, if you are worried about your weight gain, you need to quit worrying and focusing on weight (like I discuss in the body image section of this book). But, if you need to know, your weight should even out, redistribute, and lose the stored fat for healing and protection. This comes naturally. After you restore your metabolism and your body does sufficient healing, your body trusts it will not be starved again. You will not become obese or gain 300 lbs. Your appetite will settle down and your weight will stabilize.

Personally, I strongly feel it is best not to weigh yourself, or at least to not look at the number on the scale. If you desire or have a someone helping you, you can have that someone else look for you to make sure you are gaining weight, but even that is not necessary nor recommended. Why? Because it doesn't matter! You have nothing to worry about. You need to let go of the obsession around a number on a scale dictating your worth and level of health. You won't be able to judge yourself by your weight. It's triggering to see the number on the scale and can then induce a relapse, which is why I didn't weigh myself, but focused on eating a lot and not restricting my appetite, and quickly I was weight restored. You will stop gaining weight when you reach your body's optimal weight set point and are NOT restricting AT ALL anymore.

The return of your period, as a woman, is *not* a sure sign you've reached your optimal weight set point. If you still have not gotten your period, but you feel you are weight restored, you are indubitably *not* at your body's optimal weight set point yet either.

"If you relapse at the point where you feel you may be weight restored, there may be an initial phase of comfort and ease as you restrictive eating disorder begins to take hold again. I liken this situation to that of returning to an abusive partner— they are full of care, concern and apologetic pronouncements that this time will be differ-ent. It's trickery. There is no love or peace to be had with-in a restrictive eating disorder. If at any time you experi-ence a relapse, then return to your minimum intake im-mediately and seek support to keep working on applying non-restrictive behaviors of restrictive ones in response to anxieties. Your body can only be healthy at its optimal weight set point whether our society can accept that or not, is its problem, and not yours." (EDInstitue.org)

You cannot worry about a flat stomach right now and stress on if you feel bloated. You most likely feel it any time you eat, so you might as well be bloated for a good cause; you are feeding and nourishing your body, not bloated be-cause you're malnourished. You're going to be bloated for a long time, despite what you eat, because that's just one of the symptoms of recovery!

It's normal for the weight to be stored around the belly. This is as a survival mechanism the body sets in place as an extra protective layer around your most vital and vul-nerable organs in your mid-section and to prevent hy-pothermia. Sufferers of anorexia and professional dieting are expected to face an abnormal and uneven distribution of body weight, also known as "lipodystrophy", which de-posits fat to the belly and not so much the rest of the body. Your body is focusing on protecting your vital organs, as-suming you will starve it again, and without insulation around the mid-section, your organs will suffer and be in danger. Once you have been weight restored long enough, and the body trusts it will be fed consistently and not starved, the weight will redistribute. Look at the belly fat as a gold medal, rather than something to fear and feel horrible about. This shows you are recovering and winning your health and life back.

The more you keep eating consistently, the less your body will continue storing stomach fat and the quicker your body will redistribute it evenly. (and by *quick* I still mean about a year, which is the minimum, but typically, two years is to be expected). Many relapse, so don't let that be you. If you do, you will only delay your recovery longer, and the longer you must deal with recovery symptoms. Trust and be patient. Do not rush the recovery process. Do not let yourself believe after a few months you'll be ready to move on and be "normal" again when you have great damage done from over the years or even months; this belief and expectation will only set you up for disappointment. Have realistic expectations.

REST

You need to rest! Many often feel like they just want to sleep and nap all day long, facing exhaustion and fatigue, especially after meals. Don't try to justify your diet restrictions as superior because of this, since you may have felt very energized in your restrictive eating days. Starvation is shown to provoke hyperactivity. For example, these false sensations of energy surges are often compared to students deprived of sleep who display hyperactivity. It does not mean it is healthy. The fact that you're tired and fatigued is actually a good sign your body can finally communicate its needs for rest, healing, and recovery after being suppressed when in starvation mode and being restricted.

I remember, in the first several months of recovery, I would eat a meal and literally feel as if all my energy had been wiped out, drained, and the need to go lay down and take a nap. For breakfast, lunch, and dinner. But as time and recovery went on, instead of feeling tired after meals, I would feel calm, but energized, and most importantly, I would feel satisfied with brain power.

In 1900, Americans on average got nine hours of sleep a night. In 2008, we got only an average of six hours of sleep a night. Our brain and bodies were not designed to have an average 33 percent decrease in such a short while. The lightbulb is likely the cause of this change. (Dr Amen, Magnificent Mind at Any Age). Try to get at least 7-8 hours of sleep a night, even 10 would be fabulous if your schedule allows; of course more is needed for children, teens, and people on recovery.

Work on getting enough sunlight, sleep, creative outlets, fulfilling relationships, love given and received, having time to play, getting out in nature, whatever makes you so lost in the activity you could go for hours and time feels like it's just passing by so fast.

METABOLISM

We need to get your **digestion and metabolism** up and functioning again. I talk and reference a lot about metabolism in this book, because it's the main foundation for what recovery and healing is all about. It's very important for this whole process. While healing a damaged metabolism will not happen overnight, it will happen, and can happen much faster if you stop the excessive exercising, stop the restricting and avoiding foods/food groups, and eating them daily, increasing in larger increments slowly each day if needed.

Matt Stone mentions in his book *"Diet Recovery,"* *"The more you eat above your appetite and the more sedentary you are to minimize the calories you burn, the more the body fights back against this surplus by: 1-Raising the metabolism 2-Decreasing hunger 3-Increasing physical energy 4-Increasing the pulse rate 5-Increasing body temperature 6-Increasing the rate of lipolysis (burning fat for energy), and the list goes on..."*

Scott Abel in *"Understanding Metabolism,"* explains, *"A calorie is not a calorie, when looking at the big scheme of things; Instead, what really matters is the metabolic and hormonal environment of the body within which calories enter."*

Not only do you have to restore your broken and sloth-like metabolism, but restore a healthy relationship towards food to succeed. You need to get your appetite and metabolism on the same page, which will cause effortless weight-loss or restoration naturally and pain-free like any average person would.

Your body needs enough food to lose weight, even being overweight, to get back to your natural set-point weight. This is just how your daily caloric requirements, according to the Dietary Guidelines, go up as your weight goes up. If your metabolism has slowed way down from restricting and/or dieting, you may need to increase your calories and gain temporary weight to get all the biological systems functioning properly, then you can achieve your natural, healthy, and sustainable weight loss if you are indeed overweight, not just thinking you're overweight.

"We should think about our weight in terms of biology, not math. If we drink more, we urinate more. If we inhale more, we exhale more. When we eat more, our body burns more. It is proven that people who eat more have a higher metabolic rate. And this advantage is not solely theirs because you can also improve your metabolism or "heal" it after chronic dieting or an eating disorder when you start to eat enough calories. Your metabolism is suppressed by dieting and restriction, and that's why you may gain weight initially when you start to eat more, but you will drop the excess weight when the damage from your past bad eating habits is repaired and your bodily functions – hormones, hunger cues, and metabolism – are back to normal." (Oras, Elisa. BrainwashED)

Just as the body knows how to breathe unconsciously, it knows how to keep our weight within a normal range, without us having to do mathematical calculations on what to eat and how much to eat; imagine if we made mathematical calculations for how much oxygen we think our lungs should take in and at certain times, according to X,Y, and Z?! The metabolism's biological functions are too dynamic and complex, involving too many factors, for a simple one-size-fits-all mathematical determination of how many calories we should all get daily. This system can function properly and maintain our weight, without a problem if we don't tamper with the system, try to control it, try to manipulate it, and starve it. These actions on our part mess up the intuitive and instinctual process; therefore, we run into the problems we've been facing since we started restricting or dieting, whether intentionally or unintentionally (such as smoking, drinking coke spiked Coca-Cola, etc.; all of which are appetite suppressants and we begin under-eating and starving the body). A healthy and balanced body knows just how much food it needs and lets you know by hunger and satiety signals.

If, at first, in recovery, you need to count calories to make sure you are eating *enough*, then do so. Make sure not to let the counting of calories become a habit nor an obsession. If at any point you feel counting your calories stresses you out or you feel guilty or feel negative feelings if you miss a meal or day of counting calories, stop! Some people find benefit with counting calories to make sure they get enough, since they now have an altered hunger and satiety system and a brainwashed diet mindset. They don't know how much to eat and will eat too little, which will not lead to recovery success.

"Let's look at a real-life study: the Women's Health Initiative, a study that tracked nearly 49,000 women for eight years. Just as in our experiment, the women in one group ate an average of 120 fewer calories a day than the other group. Remember, that adds up to 350,400 fewer calories. How much lighter was the average woman who ate 350,400 fewer calories? The answer: 0.88 pounds. That is not a typo. Eating 350,400 FEWER calories had less than 1 percent of the impact predicted by calorie math. Eating less of a traditional Western diet does not cause a long-term fat loss because this approach incorrectly assumes that taking in fewer calories forces our body to burn fat. That has been clinically proven to be false.

Eating less does not force us to burn body fat. It forces us to burn fewer calories. That is why dieters walk around tired and crabby all day. Their bodies and brains have slowed down. When our body needs calories and none are around, it is forced to make a decision: go through all the hassle of converting calories from body fat or just slow down on burning calories. Given the choice, slowing down wins. Even worse, if we still don't have enough energy, our body burns muscle, not fat. Studies show that up to 70 percent of the non-water weight lost when people are eating less comes from burning muscle – not body fat. Only after it's cannibalized this muscle, will our body burn fat." (Jonathan Bailor, A Calorie Myth)

"This "burn more when we eat more" behavior explains how we've gained dramatically less than what would be predicted by calorie math. The "burn less when we eat less" behavior explains why studies show traditional calorie-counting approaches failing 95.4 percent of the time – and often provoking even greater rebound weight gain. When we put these two biologic behaviors together, we can see why every weight-loss study ever conducted shows that when people are given a surplus or shortage of calories, they never gain or lose the mathematically anticipated amount of fat. The body just doesn't work that way."

A good sign your metabolism is rising again is if you feel warmer than prior. A big side effect from eating disorders and dieting is low body temperature, which contributes to lowered metabolism. When you get night sweats, sweaty after meals, or just feel consistently warm or hot, or feelings of hot flashes, this is a great sign the metabolism is rising and revamping! The metabolism will balance out over time, even though it's good to keep a higher metabolism for the rest of your life. Some may be more prone to extended hotter temperatures than others, and if you were "hot blooded" before you picked up dieting, we want to get you back to that point.

That was me. I was always hot blooded. I sweated easily and frequently, but as I picked up dieting, I turned into something completely opposite and was cold all the time. I would have several layers on under a thick robe next to the fire with the heater blasting, and I was still an ice cube. That's not normal, for anyone, especially me. As I went through recovery, my body temperature picked up quickly, and every time I relapsed, my body temperature dropped again pretty dang quick.

Growing up, or in adulthood, as a response to when you say: "Oh my, I'm so sweaty!!" Or "I sweat too easily!" did people say" "Oh good, that means you're healthy!" They were right; your metabolism is working full speed and keeping your basal temperature high for optimal metabolic performance.

You get overheated, sweaty, and hot after eating a more dense and balanced meal again, because your metabolism is finally turning on and speeding up. This is good, and it won't always be like this (or you might be if you're that hot blooded person) after your body finds somewhat homeostasis and your metabolism is restored consistently for a good amount of time.

"Trying to eat less to lose weight is like trying to sleep less to do more work. You may get away with it for a short time, but it has consequences and is not sustainable. You may think that by depriving yourself of sleep you can get more work done, but when the sleep deprivation hits, you will suffer physically and mentally. It's the same with diet-induced weight loss. You cannot go against your body's biology and just decide on your own how much

you want to sleep or how much you want to weigh. If you do it that way, there will be negative after-effects.

Your body is designed to balance out automatically. The body never works against us. It doesn't want to be over-weight as much as it doesn't want to sleep more than needed. But when you constantly under-sleep, you are about to get so tired that your body forces you to sleep more. You can sleep 24 hours straight when you are seriously sleep-deprived. Same goes with weight. If you restrict food, your body forces you to binge and eat more than you normally would. When you mess with the system, it will become unbalanced, and that's why you need recovery time after eating disorders or dieting.

When we consistently eat enough calories, never restrict foods, and never try to compensate, our weight set point will get back to normal, and our body's hormonal levels will balance out. Then our body will automatically start to regulate how much to eat, when to eat, and what to eat. We simply follow our hunger cues, allow our bodies to do what they have been biologically designed to do. No calorie counting or maniacal exercise regimen to burn calories is required to stay at that healthy weight. (Oras, Elisa. BrainwashED)

Metabolism is not only used for the digestion and utilization of food stuff, but also important for many other important aspects to human health. The metabolism is in charge of things like the proper oxygenation of our cells, the energy production in the mitochondria in every one of our cells, making a healthy immune system, prolonging our youth, and so much more. Someone with a low metabolism from malnutrition feels, looks, and acts prematurely old. My grandma and I got along well spending one summer together and found we faced similar physical issues and could laugh about it, but that doesn't take away how serious and not fun it was. Yet, I got my metabolism back like it used to be after full recovery, and so can you at any age, gender, or genetic makeup.

You can revamp your metabolism at any age. I tried every healing dogma and nutritional philosophy out there, tweaking and manipulating my diet and lifestyle in so many ways. I ruined my metabolism so badly, it aged my metabolism 30 years minimum and probably more. Like I just mentioned, I literally felt like your average 80-year-old.

Start wearing the warrior "can do" mantra and ditch the victim "can't do" belief. Play more, move your body moderately, get your heart rate up, and eat decently and ENOUGH (remember, this is after the initial transition phase and whatever you need to do to get to the point where you're not living in a "dieter mentality" anymore and can have a healthy relationship with *choosing* wholesome healthy foods if and when you so desire). Eat what makes *you* feel healthy and balanced; healthy and balanced can look different for everyone.

"When metabolism falls, your sex hormone production falls (infertility, loss of sex drive, loss of period, erectile dysfunction, PMS). When metabolism falls, your youth hormone (growth hormone) falls, and you lose your ability to build muscle tissue, perform athletically, and you lose muscle tissue. When metabolism falls your rate of fat burning decreases and your body starts to manufacture more fat out of the food you eat. This causes a rise in triglycerides in your blood leading to insulin resistance (the precursor to metabolic syndrome and type 2 diabetes), increased appetite, increased storage of the food you eat into fat cells, and so forth.

When metabolism falls you produce more estrogen (both men and women) and the opposing hormones testosterone and progesterone are produced in smaller quantities. This unopposed estrogen is a prime culprit in many cancers, osteoporosis, infertility (just like taking an estrogen pill as birth control), heart disease, autoimmune disease (which women suffer from much more often than men) and countless other conditions relating to estrogen's ability to deprive cells of oxygen and energy. This of course is just the short list. When the mitochondrial energy production and respiration of every single one of your bajillion (rough estimate) cells is impaired, there is no end to how it can manifest in terms of real health problems and an overall lack of vitality." (Matt Stone, Diet Recovery)

You can often develop gastroparesis in the stomach as a survival mechanism, where the stomach churns the food longer than normal to allow the small intestine to maximize the minimal amounts of energy coming in. This doesn't stop in the stomach though; the whole gut slows to extract any and every amount of energy morsel possible to compensate for the famine. After a couple weeks to a month after consistently feeding your body as recommended, your metabolism and digestive process will begin to speed back up. Bloating, gas, pain, abdominal distention, constipation and/or diarrhea are the results when reintroducing foods. Do not let this discomfort tempt you to go on a fast or restrict food types and overall food intake again. This is one reason I outlined the meal plan I provide in my MasterCourse for 6-7 meals a day, rather than 3 square meals a day, to help ease this discomfort a little. Otherwise, if you feel it no matter what, you might as well not stretch out your meals if you desire to eat more at meal times, rather than smaller meals every few hours. That's up to you. When the metabolism rises, food passes through the digestive tract more briskly.

I want to make a brief mention about Candida, since I fell
into that trap as well and tried every diet manipulation,
candida cleanse, sugar free, starch free, herbal protocol to
try to "kill" the candida, and it all only broke my bank and
made my health worse with no change. Candida will balance out once your internal ecosystem balances out and
you strengthen your metabolism, repair your organs, and
build your immune system again.

Once you're able to metabolize your sugars and glucose
more efficiently, there will be no need for the candida levels to rise to compensate for the extra sugar in the blood.
Also, movement, walks, or any preferred source of moder-
ate exercise each day or every couple days will help burn
off excess sugars in the blood, which also helps with candida levels rising. (But as a reminder, don't exercise in the
beginning of recovery to compensate for the extra sugars
in the blood or so called candida "flare ups." People will
find any excuse to restrict again or why they can exercise
before the time is right.)

When you starve your body, you not only starve the cells
and tissues of your body, but you starve the most critical
gut bacteria of their fuel; you also lower your digestive enzyme levels. Since there are about the same number of bacterial cells in the human body as human cells, which there
are about 10 trillion cells, you can see how detrimental it is
to our health if they die off.

Full fat yogurt with the live cultures helps tremendously.
Sauerkraut, because of the cruciferous raw veggie factor,
can cause more discomfort, which is why yogurt is better
recommended, but again, try what works for you. Because
you have lowered your digestive enzyme production from
lowering your metabolism from starvation, you can experience the symptoms of "lactose intolerance," even if you

never were prior to your restrictiveness and eating disorder. This is because your digestive system is stressed in the current condition it's in. It no longer can consistently produce the lactase enzyme to break down the lactose.

If so, you can again digest lactose in the future if you are consistent with your recovery. In the meantime, since the lactose is hard to break down, you might notice fermented dairy products are better handled, such as cheese, yogurt, sour cream, kefir, cultured butter, and ghee (not fermented, just the milk solids are boiled out, leaving you with pure butter oil only). This is because, during the fermentation process, the bacteria eats up the lactose as its fuel; therefore, lactose is only minimal in very minute amounts, if any at all. And if you heard, "We are the only species that consumes another species' milk" this is actually simply untrue, as in nature, many animals partake in other animals' milk when they can; it is highly nutritious.

EXCUSES, CON-TROL, AND CHANGE

Stop waiting, procrastinating, and making excuses why you can't or won't recover now. There's no better time like the present and waiting any longer will only make things worse. You have already given too big of a chunk of your life to your DE, and it's not worthy of another day. Realize, your DE played a role in your life thus far, but now, it no longer serves you. It's time to let go and move on to better things. You're better than this. You deserve happiness, healthiness, and freedom. You're worthy of this. No one deserves to be in a prison of a restrictive eating disorder. Have enough respect for yourself to treat yourself and your body as a temple and to dedicate your time to recover and get healthy. Promise yourself you're going to stick through it and don't allow yourself to break the promise. Do something for your sanity for once in your life.

This is not for anyone else but you and your quality of life. What do you have to lose? I'm sure your life and how you're feeling now is not so pleasant, and things can only go up from here (after the recovery symptoms). Trust me; the other side of recovery is infinite in how much better and more pleasing it is to live free from disordered eating. Just remember, nothing in life worth having comes easy. Health is earned, not given freely. But you have the power to push through. I have 100% faith in you.

The more tightly you grip your "control" around yourself, food, exercise, weight, body image, whatever, the harder you swing in the other direction eventually. Restriction and control are not the answer to your food problems. You need to **let go of control** and be open to new ideas, guidance, and advice. We will always have an influence, but we can never have complete control over anything.

"New information causes you to change your behavior; that is the sign of intelligent life. It takes a bit of effort but you are worth the time it takes." (Daniel Amen M.D., Magnificent Mind At Any Age).

Be okay with vulnerability and letting go of control, so someone else can help you. I would have gotten there much quicker with less setbacks and problems if I had gotten help or guidance from others sooner. Now is the time to accept help in your life and trust whatever or whoever it is. It's okay to ask for help. This is your ego, pride, and ED talking, because it still wants to be in control. But where has that led you? Nowhere pretty, obviously, and it's time to challenge these thoughts.

Realizing you don't have to do everything in life alone will liberate and help you accomplish more. It shows character and wisdom to swallow your pride and ask for help, let go of your complete control, and admit you don't have to do everything alone. I learned that along the way. The moment I was forced to let go was the moment I broke the habit and a new door opened. It was scary and uncomfortable, but it promoted and activated a shift of great change I so desperately needed.

Being alone in recovery can be a setup for relapse or relapsing more than necessary. I relapsed far past what's normal and delayed my recovery by many months when I no longer had the support from my friends in Hawaii after the first few weeks of initiating recovery with them. It's helpful to have support of someone who understands and can hold you accountable, so you don't revert when the temptation kicks in or the battle in your mind kicks in. It's also important for you to get out of your mind, take the stress off yourself, and hand over your control to an outside source for guidance in the beginning, at least until you have enough brain power and understanding to proceed forward on your own.

STRESS AND GRATEFULNESS

Stop stressing out and obsessing about what goes into your mouth and accept that you need food and lots of it to get better. Get over the fat-phobia, the carb-phobia, the starch-phobia, the dairy-phobia, the grain-phobia, or whatever "intolerance" you decided you had at the start of your restrictive behaviors. Pick up some bread or some cheese and eat it guilt, stress, worry, and anxiety free. If you can't, then you need to work on this ASAP.

Starving yourself is one of the biggest stressors you could put on your body, and stress itself (in any situation) makes you gain weight, and more than needed if you were to deviate off your diet, exercise regime, restrictions, or just by simply eating more. When stress goes down, metabolism goes up.

"Stress is a silent killer and a thief of millions of people's dreams. It's something worth noting that a feeling of gratitude actually raises DHEA which counteracts cortisol. So instead of stressing on the things you're dealing with, how can you find something to be grateful for, even the things that are stressing you out right now; it's by looking at the benefits of what's actually happening. Far too often we look at something that happens to us and we consider it to be bad. Rather than asking the question, "what is the benefit of this?" Hindsight is a beautiful thing, but is often brought in 2 months, 2 years, 6 months where people look back at a bad event and then see the benefits moving forward. Then they go, "you know what, I'm so glad that happened!" But imagine if you can bring hindsight into the present moment, where you can be

173

grateful for the things that are happening, bad and good, moment to moment, which will naturally increase your gratitude; naturally increase your DHEA and diminish the effects of cortisol and stress they can have on the body. If you can count your blessings, you can create more." (Kerwin Rae).

Be grateful for what you have, and I'm sure, no matter what situation you're in, you can always find something to be grateful for. I'm grateful I am mobile and still able to get up and walk around. I'm grateful for my eyesight to see the beauty in the world. I'm grateful for my hearing to hear my favorite music and nature sounds. I'm grateful to have a family who loves me unconditionally. I'm grateful to have a car to drive me where I need to go, but also have my legs that allow me to walk if I decide to. I'm grateful to live where I do and have the freedom of speech and thought I have. I'm grateful for my dog who gives me unconditional love and entertainment. I'm grateful to have had all the experiences I've had to teach me what I need to know to grow and challenge myself. I'm grateful for so many things, and I know you can find something too. Have an attitude of gratitude. Try this exercise with your daily meditation or prayer, or whatever your daily practice is, write down 3 things you're grateful for. I'm serious. That simple.

Dr. Amen, a renowned medical doctor who performs SPECT scans on the brain to show activity and inactivity in different areas of the brain, "has proof from these brain scans, that negative thinking actually shuts down the coordination part of the brain. After preforming different SPECT scans on her client, the first time she was scanned after meditating on all the things she was thankful for in her life. Several days later she was then scanned after focusing on the major fears in her life. After the "appreciation mediation," her brain looked very healthy. On the day of her "fear-based-meditation" her brain showed serious overall decreased activity in two parts of her brain. Her cerebellum in the pack part of the brain, completely shut down. The cerebellum is involved in physical coordination such as walking and playing sports, as well as processing speed and how quickly we can integrate new information. When the cerebellum experiences low activity, people tend to be clumsier and less likely to think their ways out of problems. They think and process information more slowly and they get confused more easily. The other area of the brain that was affected was the temporal lobes, especially on the left. The temporal lobes are involved with mood, memory, and temper control. Problems in this part of the brain are associated with some forms of depression and dark thoughts, violence, and memory problems. When the client practiced gratitude, her temporal lobes looked healthy and not overstimulated; when she frightened herself with negative and fearful thoughts, her temporal lobes became much less active. Negative thought patterns change the brain in a negative way. Practicing gratitude literally helps you have a brain to be grateful for." (Daniel Amen M.D., Magnificent Mind At Any Age).

EDEMA

I have a whole section on this, because it is most concerning and anxiety inducing symptom to recoveries. I was horrified from it, until I understood why it was necessary...

I'm talking about the Edema that **hurts**. It aches, it makes you look and feel pregnant, and makes your eyes and face look puffy. I had such horrible edema that it was too painful to even stand or walk on my feet. I couldn't even bend or cross my legs without them feeling as if they would burst and explode. It was a swollen achy feeling but was severely uncomfortable. I cried to my dad one day about how frustrated I felt because of how painful it was to walk to the bathroom from my room. I cried to myself much more often in private (I'm one who used to show my emotions rarely, no matter how upset I was with what I was going through. If the emotions came out around others, I just couldn't hold it in any longer, and it often came out of nowhere, so this was big). This went on for a couple months for me, not just the couple weeks most claim it will last. This was scary for me because I thought something was going horribly wrong, thinking, "Why is it lasting for so many months?!" But low and behold, it cleared up!

This is not meant to scare you, but to prepare you, if your symptoms are lasting longer than expected, and to stick through it. Do not let what the edema makes you look like or feel like send you back to a relapse like it did me often. Let this be your warning, so you can expect what's coming and not let it panic you into quitting.

Your body does not care about vanity right now!

Edema is an important part to recovery, although it can be scary, uncomfortable, painful, annoying, and make you feel not so beautiful. It should not be feared nor suppressed. Embrace it; it *will* go away. And don't freak out at this news of water weight gain. This is just so you know what's happening. *Knowledge is power*; knowledge can prevent relapses so you stick through the symptoms, knowing they are not permanent or signs your body's failing you; these are good signs your body is doing its job and *healing*!

Think about if you stubbed your toe, twisted and ankle, or tweaked your finger, and they ache, hurt to touch, swell up, and are inflamed. These are symptoms that your body is signaling to you *to stay off the inflamed area and rest*; these are signs your body is *healing* that area. The swelling is water retention, and the pain is a reaction of the tissues/nerves to the swelling, which sends these signals to stay off. The water retention from disordered eating recovery is fluid being retained in areas of the body where damage of overworked and depleted tissues is being dealt with, nourished, healed, strengthened, and recovered. The fluid being retained helps to speed up the recovery process because the cells and nutrients can travel faster on this terrain.

Remember the soreness and pain are signals from the body to REST and to keep you immobile so you do not re-injure yourself, create more damage, or take away necessary energy needed for the urgent healing. Edema, soreness, pain, inflammation is your warrior trophy, your healing badge of honor.

Not only did I relapse a couple times back into restricting, but I allowed myself to take strong kidney and diuretic herbs and prescription diuretics to flush the water. NO! Please do not do this! Your body is holding on to the water for a reason, so don't flush it out. Flushing it out will only create more problems and extend your recovery time. When you flush out the fluid and water retention with diuretics, you flush away your chances at recovering and healing.

If the swelling is too painful, try ice packs on and off for 20 minutes at a time, or you can consider compression socks and garments to ease the pain, but don't stop the healing process.

One of the main reasons you retain water and gain real meat and fat on you, on less than optimal amounts of food intake is because *your metabolism is suppressed!* But, don't think your metabolism is ruined and broken. This is a survival mechanism your metabolism has adapted to keep you alive during starvation bouts. The metabolism slows down to extract any bit of nutrition it can from the scarce calories coming in and stores it as fat for the famine and potential future famine.

When you restrict, either through not eating enough and/ or over exercising, your body, to keep you alive and existing, stops all biological functions it can to save energy and takes energy from fat tissue, bones, muscles, organs, nerves, etc., to fill the void. This is done through lowering the metabolic rate. The body will be "thrifty" and conservative when in starvation mode and will not raise the metabolic rate when you are only feeding it 1,000 to less than 2,000 calories a day; it will take whatever extra energy and calories that would normally go to biological functions to replenish fat tissue. These conservation techniques are done to prevent organ failure in cold weather. (Note how sensitive to being cold you get when malnourished or on a restrictive regime.) I got the most cold-sensitive in my Orthorexic phase; I turned into a (barely) living and breathing icicle.

You need higher food intakes to provide energy for physical repair and not just for restoring your weight. You cannot repair all the damage from restriction and dieting and enter full and permanent remission without sufficient intakes of food, although you can restore only your weight with sub-optimal caloric intake.

The issue here is not whether you are *clinically* underweight, but whether what your body deems as your optimal weight "set-point" for the time being, and whether you are under or over it. BMI sucks, don't listen to it, don't go by it. Even my Therapist told me this in recovery and thereafter. BMI doesn't consider so many necessary factors to determine whether you are healthy. It's a BMI lie.

We can easily gain more in water than we lose in fat yielding a net gain in weight. Water weighs more than fat. This is important to understand because water weight and edema when recovering can also be why you weigh so much and gain 15 pounds in the first couple of days or week of your eating recovery plan. This is the edema, not real weight gain. If you say, "my weight gain" seems too fast, too unique, too much, etc., it's as expected, the retention of water.

As you experience all this, answer your questions for yourself and know what is happening when you ask: "Am I almost done with my recovery because I'm almost or at my "normal weight?" (NO); "Am I going to become obese?" (NO); Am I a glutton or greedy for eating more now? (*rolls eyes* NO!!); Will my weight gain ever slow down?" (YES) or things like this.

Rapid weight changes always represent losses or gains in water weight. (Hence, people on ketogenic and low-carb diets lose weight so quickly in the first week or two; for every 1 gram of carbohydrate (or glycogen), you have 3-4 grams of water stored in the muscles. Carbohydrates store more water in the body and help to prevent dehydration. This is good. Water is so important for our survival; we are about 60% water as adults and even higher as infants, so quit with the diuretics (herbal diuretics included!).

Another note on edema, look closely at a baby, who is puffy and fatty and looks like a mini sumo-wrestler (oh, wait, was that just me?) They have major edema around the face, arms, legs, toes, and all over. They're just a blob of soft water and fat it seems like, right? That water retention is necessary for quickly delivering all the nutrients coming in for the most crucial time of development... same with us recoveries; we must pudge up, retain water, look soft and as if we have edema. This water retention has purpose for our bodies taking in all the nutrients finally coming in and needing to deal with them quickly to repair the damage and deficit ASAP. You need to repair the damaged skin, nails, hair, digestive system, kidneys, bones, blood, brain (about 1,000 calories per day); on top of this, you have to maintain daily functions such as breathing, heart beating, your basal metabolic rate (another 1,000 calories). You also need about 1,000 calories *per day* just going towards the actual fat and muscle rebuilding. With all this, you better dang well be supplying the calories daily for your body to carry out these functions; the less you eat, thinking *you* don't need 3,000+ calories a day in recovery, the longer it will take you to recover. The harder it is on your body to repair the damage without sufficient energy to do so.

If you go through a couple mini-relapses throughout the beginning of your recovery, (which almost everyone does) don't let it be the end all, be all. Become stronger with each relapse, but try to have the fewest relapses possible. Relapsing is not even worth it. Be prepared for several rebound edema days. Each relapse creates more damage that the body now must go back and fix. Your body will handle this and go back to where you were in your recovery after these several days of edema and you being diligent on your rest and meals.

INTUITIVE EXER-CISE

I'm fairly certain Madilyn Moon and I agree on this area, if not the rest of the book too. Have you heard of her? Ex Fitness Model that found sanity after ditching the fitness modeling and competing world, like myself? She's a rockstar, who has dedicated her time not only to helping people all around the globe to quit the dieting and restriction madness, but also to empower people to stop being the perfectionist, accept themselves, love their bodies, and honor their lifestyles by living out their true passions in life. Anyway, she's great, so check her out too. Okay back to this exercise stuff...

It's so important to lay off the exercise, altogether, no exceptions in the first phase of recovery. I recommend not working out for at least the first month minimum, and only then if you've consistently not relapsed or restricted. If you're still having strong cravings for food and having binges and still feel that ravenous hunger, then you should wait until that settles down, waiting up to 6 months or longer, for you to work out at all if need be.

The first month, I recommend you just rest a lot, like you're on vacation from everything health and fitness. Naps, massages, resting, reading, journaling, sleep as much as you can, you got it? Don't even go on long walks or hikes. You need to accept that your body needs you to rest, physically, mentally, and emotionally. Spend a lot of time sitting with your feet elevated, lying down, or whatever position suits your fancy.

After the first month or so, perhaps even 3, you can incorporate light yoga classes or light walks or hikes outside to get fresh air, sunlight, and to surround yourself in nature. If that's triggering though, and even these make you have thoughts to overdo it, push yourself, and you want to exercise only for the sake to "burn calories" or "to lose the weight you've gained," or any other disordered thoughts around these simple exercises, then don't do it. It should be for joy only, and because you want to move your body lightly, and that's it.

Exercise is for healthy people that have no history of disordered eating or over exercising, or who are weight restored and later into their recovery. Even then, with our past of extreme behaviors, we need to cool it and keep an eye on our exercise habits. Don't let your mind convince you that exercise is healthy and necessary for you right now in the beginning of recovery. Mood enhancing, endorphin releasing benefits that most justify as the main reasoning for them wanting to exercise in the beginning of recovery can instead be achieved through simply sitting outside in nature with fresh air, listening to the surrounding sounds. This is scientifically backed up.

Because of malnutrition, your body is in a stressed state and your cortisol levels will be through the roof in recovery. If you try to over-consume calories to compensate for your extra energy expenditures through exercise (against the suggestions), your body will focus the energy to repairs and storing the extra energy for weight restoration, rather than using it to support the extra work you've done. This is understandable for your body just being extra conservative at this delicate time.

If you continue to exercise in recovery, you will stay in a semi-starvation state. You may not fully recover, and you might even over-shoot your set weight point because your body is still in semi-starvation mode and thinks it needs to keep saving for the continual energy deficit and for the next restrictive episode. In the Minnesota Experiment, men with the largest calorie increase in the rehabilitation period recovered the quickest; on average, the subjects gained 140% more fat than they had prior to the experiment, which went back to normal over time. People who go through recovery on lower amounts of calories will end up with more fat on their body after recovery than people who go into full recovery on proper amounts of foods.

Again, this was me; I kept fighting the recovery process and wanted to revert to being strict, and "pure", and "clean," and "healthy," from my ED's dogmas and beliefs. Initially, I reached my set weight point and stop gaining, but then I restricted again. I kept going back and forth from restricting to recovery amounts and types of food, to restricting again, to binging, to exercising again, and this went on for months. So, I put on far more weight than I should have, because each time I restricted again, my body stored more and more. My body still felt threatened and remained in a semi-starved place, which led it to believe it needed to keep storing for the next restriction.

Avoid bouncing back and forth from recovery to restricting; that's why I say you have to commit 100%! If you keep trying to restrict in recovery, your body can't relax and feel comfortable enough to come out of the semi-starved mode. Until the body thinks the famine is over and food is abundant, it won't stop storing, and it won't come out of starvation mode. Never deny your body of food when it is asking for it and whatever it's asking for. Tell your body, "If you are hungry, I will feed you." Show your body it won't be starved again, and that you will be consistently feeding it anytime it asks for fuel and nourishment; earn back that trust slowly.

I worked with someone maintaining a normal weight after the initial weight restoration and for several months she still could not get her period to return. She got a gnarly injury finally from exercising, which forced her to have to rest with no activity. Within less than a month, her period returned, and all was history. This was proof to her and I that, without proper rest (no activity at all), the menstrual cycle cannot return.

After you're well into your recovery, not having binges anymore, and can eat intuitively, living life without your restrictive eating disorder running the show, exercise will be a fantastic experience. I love to exercise! I love to challenge myself. I love how it makes me feel, but I'm able to exercise now without feeling guilty if I miss a day or week or month of exercise. I'm able to stop the workout if my body is telling me its fatigued and it wants to rest. I'm able to rest when I'm drained and have no desire to be active some days. But what's cool is I have boundless amounts of energy now from all the fuel I feed my body, specifically starchy carbohydrates and saturated fats. I can now do all the exercises I once couldn't do (yes, I'm even referring to my competing/fitness model days). I looked aesthetically fit, but on the inside, I was weak. I could barely do squats or many leg exercises correctly with the bursts of energy I have now, because I was so depleted and restricted. Now, I can do all the leg exercises and other exercises that require bursts of energy to complete the reps or to carry out the needed extended stamina to keep pushing, and I feel energized after! But some days, I have no desire to do these exercises, and I respect that. This is huge for me.

I also know what kind of exercising I like to do. Not what the biggest fitness trend is, but what I enjoy. And that changes. I get bored after I do a certain way of exercising for so long, and when I feel the need to switch it up, I have other outlets to turn to. This prevents plateaus or stopping exercise because of boredom or hatred for the exercises. Not everyone wants to do headstands and yoga all day, not everyone wants to go to a stinky stuffy gym with a bunch of people in a tight enclosed space (okay, not all gyms are like that), not everyone likes to cycle or ride bikes, not everyone likes to play basketball, not everyone likes to run long distance, not everyone likes HIIT (high intensity interval training), not everyone likes Zumba or Bootcamp classes, not everyone likes to work out in the morning, and same with the evening. But if you do truly love and enjoy one of these or one of the MANY kinds of fitness, do it, and enjoy it, and find others who share the same enjoyment of that activity. Find *your* fitness.

And yea, I'll push myself with whatever I'm doing to a healthy amount of exhaustion, so I'm breathing hard, sweating, and heart's pounding. But when my body tells me it's done, I'm done. I listen and respect the temples wishes. My body is my temple; my body is my guide. You don't want to get comfortable with the exercises but you want to push harder and challenge yourself to get better each time. No easy way out here, either. This is just like with anything else in life; just find *your* balance and find *your* limits.

This is what intuitive exercise and a healthy relationship with being active looks like. You could be the most physically flexible yogi but the most internally inflexible human being ever. Have you ever encountered these uptight yogi sticklers? I have. Not very Namaste or Zen status. And this is not limited to the yoga realm; I've seen this in every fitness category, weight lifting, cycling, running, you name it. This is where Westernized yoga practices fail; Eastern yoga practices emphasize the internal exercise work even more than the physical, sometimes. A lot (not all) of western yoga practices decided the focus on internal work, wasn't as important for our physically and externally aesthetically obsessed culture and has been often left out. We are left with another exercise fad like *Tae Bo* or *The Shake Weight*. You need to work on both aspects. Do the physical exercise for healthful purposes and helping your mental world. The work on your internal world will then help your physical world. They are connected, and when there is an imbalance, it's hard to seek true fitness success.

INTUITIVE EATING

If your weight seems stable, if you have gotten your period back for 3 consecutive months in a row, if you have continued to eat minimum amounts of food, and it is comfortable to do so for several months, if your hair is not brittle or falling out anymore, if you're no longer cold, tired, and achy anymore, if you are no longer retaining water, if you are sleeping well, or things of this nature, these are good signs you may be ready to attempt to listen and follow your hunger cues and practice intuitive eating. If you are overly confident on being able to eat by only hunger cues, this may mean you're actually away from remission still as the sure sign would look more like you are questioning whether you should start eating according to hunger cues, but are still iffy and anxious about the fact of whether you can trust yourself.

What other species on the planet takes the time to stress about what they can or cannot eat that day or the rest of their lives? What other creatures turn their meals into math equations? So, 'Dana the Deer' and 'Gerard the Giraffe' heard the news from the new "guru" down by the watering hole, 'Luke the Lion,' that says any green food is the food that makes us fat and sick, and we need to stay away from those foods! So, Dana and Gerard restrict and count their calories of leaves and bugs to fit their macros for the day; they eat what Luke is eating, even if that food disgusts them and makes them feel horrible. This sounds silly. Super silly and lame. Because it is. Dieting, restricting, tracking for humans is also silly and lame. They don't diet or restrict, or even think twice about what and how much they eat. They just eat to their satisfaction and satiety cues and move on with their freakin' life and enjoy the simplicity, chores, and playfulness life offers.

We're in a world where logic is valued over intuition. We are so up in our heads and not in our hearts, our full bodies, or a balance between it all, which creates imbalance indefinitely. We over think, we over analyze, and we over obsess. There is so much mental anguish going on because we are not trusting ourselves. We used to depend upon intuition, and now, we pretend it's not there, or that following intuition means we're foolish. Instead of having laundry lists of good or bad foods, following the latest fads or trends, we need to check in with ourselves for what we really need right now. With trusting your intuition, what is more freeing than being your own guide? Instead of listening to the world on how you should live, you're now listening to yourself. This is true and authentic freedom.

Between each individual, we should take in the best of certain information and put our own twist to make it work for our own needs and situation. Aren't you tired of living by someone else's orders and doctrines? Don't you want to live your own life again? Aren't you sick of not feeling free, and losing your mind because of it?

Guru's.... *"If you believe you 'need' health, you'll be controlled and potentially manipulated by the people you believe hold the keys to greater health. If you need nothing, you can't be controlled." Kerwin Rae.* Don't depend on others for all the answers to *your* questions and problems anymore. It's time to look within and trust yourself again. It's nice to have guidance, learn from others, and hear their opinions and beliefs, but you have to find what resonates with you; your situation is always unique, and *you* must determine what's best for you.

Stop only listening to everyone else, even if they speak against what you are doing or want to do. They are probably only speaking against it, because they too are in the restrictive dieting bubble of their own from the media and conditioning. They want to keep you down, because they feel envy, jealousy, or resentment to everyone else around them who can enjoy food and life more than they can. You are allowing yourself to eat again, and because they aren't, they want to hold you down to their level; if they can't do it, nobody should. You need to learn not to always people please, but please yourself and your needs over others if it is for your health and wellbeing.

"One of the biggest obstacles to maverick thinking is the powerful desire to be accepted by our peer group. The need to belong, to be part of a group of family, friends, and colleagues, is hardwired in our brain. When we venture out on our own, when we think independently for ourselves, we risk rejections or ridicule from the group we love. When we cooperate with others the pleasure circuits light up, even when it costs us money. It feels good to get along.

On the surface, the researchers argue that cooperation and altruism is a good thing, an adaptive social skill. I agree that it certainly can be. But it can also be a terrible thing and cause you to lose yourself if you cooperate so much that you have no idea what your own thoughts are.

Cooperation, according to this study, works in the same areas of the brain implicated in addictions. It is so important for some of us to be cooperative that we allow our husbands or wives to control us, belittle us, sometimes abuse us; we stay in jobs that are not a good fit for us, because we "just want to get along"; we ignore underperforming employees because we do not want to confront them; we allow our children to get away with bad behavior, because we want them to like us. When cooperation gets out of hand, it is similar to an addiction. It generates anxiety and such thought as "please love me, no matter what"; "don't be mad at me"; "I'll do anything to get you back"; and "I'll do anything to get along." The anxiety becomes too intense to deal with the problems, so you go along to get along. The anxiety can prevent you from speaking your mind even thinking your own thoughts. It is part of the reason that rigid religions and cults flourish.

It seems that we need a balance between enough serotonin so that we feel good and can be flexible and cooperative, without going overboard and losing our identity to the will of the group. You need some angst to know when things are not right. Over control, dependence, anxiety, and stress also inhibit independent thinking. Parents, teachers, or managers who over control or demand "blind" compliance, often work against themselves. Whenever you demand sameness or blind compliance, you lock the independent minds away and do not hear what they are thinking. You limit your growth.

When other people demand that you think the way they do, your mind no longer has to work, and if you are lazy, you simply comply. Or you may get mad and start pushing against them, actively sabotage them, or walk away. Over control, dependence, and anxiety is a common dynamic ruining people and inhibiting the individuals independent thinking and creativity. Going along just to get along, especially when things are not right, is harmful and often demoralizing." (Daniel Amen M.D., Magnificent Mind At Any Age).

In the same way, we follow what others are doing, or are asking of us, or are expecting of us, just to please others, get along, avoid conflict, or avoid confrontation. We stay quiet or act in a manner *like the rest,* so we don't stand out or draw attention to us. What if we were just to follow our thoughts, ask questions, and challenge the norm, embrace our true selves, stand up for ourselves, and be firm (not argumentative) in our beliefs and viewpoints, even if it is against the "norm" of society?

We would be much happier and have more internal success if we just believed in ourselves that we can think for ourselves and know what works for us, makes us feel our best, and what does not. It may be easier to go with what people want or tell you to do to make them happy or feel at ease, but eventually, you will feel frustrated, resentful, and set yourself up for abuse (emotional and/or physical), heartbreak, anxiety, feeling of emptiness, and lack of original thought.

Rudolf Flesch wrote in his book *Why Johnny Can't Read*, *"creative thinking may mean simply the realization that there's no particular virtue in doing things the way they always have been done."* Independent thinkers tend not to follow the rules just because others think they should; they do not go with the group "norm" just because there is a criterion. Sometimes, you must take a different approach from the typically accepted and standard one, even if it means doing what is difficult. Be patient and have hope; if you have lost your voice or intuition, know it is definitely possible to find it again.

Okay lets get back on topic to Intuitive Eating. Most of us know you cannot be healthy without acknowledging nutrition as part of your healthy lifestyle. However, I must make known that, if the information for a healthy diet is presented to two people, one with a healthy relationship with food and one who does not, it's difficult for the person without a healthy relationship with food to benefit from a healthy diet. These "professional dieters" can take and embody the guidelines to the extreme and make what is otherwise healthful diet guidelines into yet another stressful "diet."

Intuitive eating is not necessarily your golden ticket to junk food freedom. It doesn't mean you *have* to listen to every craving and anything that's in sight, unless you want to. It's more about listening to all aspects of yourself, your body, your brain, and your emotions, and finding a balance within it all by tuning in and listening to all of them.

Just because you're deciding to let go of the restrictiveness and not care so much, doesn't mean you *have* to go buck-wild and go through the drive-thru every waking moment (or maybe you do). It's more that if you have the cookie, you're well aware it has refined sugar, flour, and less than ideal vegetable oils (like soybean oil), but you'll be *a-o-kay* with that indulgence whenever you decide to. You won't have to binge on mounds of cookies now, simply because you "feel you've failed on your diet," and now just give up for the day, week, month... These thoughts should not be there at this point!! No shame! No guilt! EVER. NADA.

There is nothing wrong with eating junk foods, so you don't feel restricted and stressed, but there is also nothing wrong with wanting to incorporate healthful, wholesome foods in your diet, as well, because they make you feel good. There is nothing wrong with saying no to a food because you simply have no desire for it. A balance within your diet can help you feel more balanced overall, which means you can have a stress-free relationship with eating and be overall more happy, healthy, and calm. Eat healthy wholesome foods to nourish your body, but also eat any other foods you crave to nourish your mind and soul — find your balance.

Just because something is not considered "healthy" to society doesn't mean it's not serving a purpose for you or within your body. It is serving a purpose for you in your heart that makes you feel great! Maybe it's allowing you to connect with an old best friend again, your mom, or sister.

Maybe it's a good memory you get to experience again; for example bagels and cream cheese or pasta was your favorite food growing up or maybe you shared some memorable bonding times with a parent over this specific meal, and now you're able to feel their presence and that positive memory again when you eat that food. If you know you're more of an emotional eater (because we all are emotional eaters at some point, and it's not always a bad thing!) versus a restrictive dieter, Isabel Foxen Duke is the expert on helping people deal with emotional eating and binge eating disorders. If you're feeling more on that side of the spectrum, I highly recommend checking out her work.

The thing with raw foods versus cooked foods or intermittent fasting or eating breakfast/after 6pm is solely a preference thing and should not be a tell-all be-all for everybody. If you prefer raw salads or fruits vs sautéed veggies or stewed fruits, then that should be the determining factor for if you should eat more raw veggies vs cooked veggies. It doesn't mean you have to be a 100% raw foodist, nor a raw vegan, just because of the preference of raw salads versus cooked veggies or cooling foods. Apparently there really are different bodily constitutions that do better with certain temperatures and processing of foods or different food groups according to Ayruveda and the 3 Doshas (Kapha, Pitta, Vata). The problem with this is people may take the suggestions to the extreme for each Dosha as finite, and they feel they have to follow everything to the T with no flexibility. In reality, they should just take the suggestions and tailor it to their unique needs. There is much wisdom we can learn from each of the many healing modalities in the world. But instead of following each with no adjustments and integrating many to fit your own, people think they can only follow one way at a time because of the many contradictions between modalities. This is simply untrue, and you should take what you want and leave the rest. Or better yet, get away from seeking outside of yourself altogether. I have noticed within my relationships just how different all our different food preferences are; instead of taking it personally if we don't agree on food preferences, I've learned to accept our differences. We need to honor each other's preferences.

Another example goes for the "intermittent fasting" bandwagon; if you wake up one day and are just not hungry in the morning or don't get hungry until 10 or 11 or 12 o'clock, then cool; listen to your hunger signals and don't force yourself to eat. But if you wake up the next day and you are hungry and thinking about food at 6am or 8am or you're hungry past 6pm, you should definitely not deprive yourself just because you have taken on the role of being an "intermittent faster." And this may change from day to day.

With all this said, you shouldn't be thinking about implementing any recommendations from different modalities until you are recovered. Once you are recovered and have recovered your hunger and satiety signals and have been practicing intuitive eating, then you'll be able to decipher when and *if* (not recommended) to integrate these different philosophies to your own needs if you so desire. If you try to prematurely in your recovery, you will set yourself up for a relapse and become obsessive and restrictive, tuning out your intuition for when and what to eat.

If you are truly an intuitive eater, though, you won't seek these modalities for what you need or want to eat. You'll just be able to notice the foods you're drawn to or that your body is craving.

You know that person you're always envious over, because they can "eat whatever they want and lots of it" and not gain a pound, and you're sitting over here losing your sanity from restricting, and feeling physically ill from the same meal? Well, that's no longer serving you to feel that way, and it's time to make a change, because I'll tell ya, restricting is not the way to health and freedom.

You shouldn't be psyching yourself out to where you will have a panic attack from something in your meal you've ordered or your loved one made for you. You should be able to indulge guilt free, whenever, wherever, and whatever it is, thanksgiving desert, Aunt Joe's pie, bff's dinner, drive thru meal on a road-trip, you name it, and it should be willingly and lovingly embraced. Go out to the restaurant and get exactly what you want, not what you think you "should" get and be envious about what others around you ordered and are enjoying. Don't "should" on yourself. It's just pointless. And when you get what you ordered, don't say, "Oh no, I shouldn't be doing this..." Nope, just enjoy it guilt-free and full of pleasure.

Again, here's that kickass chick leading the way for fighting emotional eating and empowering women/men all over the world, named Isabel Foxen Duke, in her free video course series *"Stop Fighting Food"*; "Think about the most normal eater you know. Family, friend, random person you see regularly, it doesn't matter. This person can naturally eat a normal amount of food, follows their hunger cues and satiety, who has a normal body type, not really thinking about what, when, why, how much, they're eating, or trying too hard. Who is just relaxed around food? What are they doing that you're not? How are they thinking, that you're not thinking? What is their relationship with food that's different than yours? What's going on in their *mind* around food or over exercising or their body? It's changing the *thinking*, not the behaviors (will power, restriction) around food, that's going to allow you to create a normal relationship with food. The difference is not will power between you and this person; normal eaters are not trying to control themselves around food all the time. They naturally don't want to eat an entire jar of peanut butter, or a couple loafs of bread in one sitting, because it would make them feel sick."

These people are not thinking of food all day, about what they're going to eat next, and what food they cannot eat next. They may plan a lunch for work or school the next day, but they don't over-plan and stress about what they're putting in their lunch; they don't think about the food they get to eat the next day, all night long, salivating in their sleep.

Why do people feel so badly about themselves when they break their diet? Because they feel really uncomfortable with gaining weight or maintaining weight. Most people are not okay with the way they *eat* because of the way they *look*. Shame and guilt around food or how you weigh almost always results in binge eating. So, even the feeling of being fat or feeling bad about our bodies can trigger a binge or a day(s) without eating at all, depending on how the person copes. When a person's weight doesn't dictate their self-esteem, they don't feel guilt and shame around food and, therefore, don't binge or starve themselves. Normal eaters do not care so much; they don't waste their thoughts on it. Changing your relationship with your body is the mandatory prerequisite to being able to change your relationship with food." (Isabel Foxen Duke, Stop Fighting Food).

If one relies on "willpower" on its own, there'll come a day where your willpower is overpowered by the practical sense of your intelligent body, in efforts to survive; the other option is death from malnutrition or ill health problems. People are instinctively choosing the most metabolic raising foods whilst in the post-diet binge period. Lowering your metabolism with a diet makes you crave more calorie dense foods, particularly calorie dense, concentrated sources of salt, starch, fat, and sugar combined into one. Don't get me started on "The Pleasure Trap." This is not a failure in willpower. It's simply our species' evolutionary adapted intelligence banning your brain's foolish idiocy.

So, *what is a healthy relationship with food?* It's simply seeing food as fuel and nourishment for our body to live out other and more important daily tasks. It's fuel to help us continue living out our life purpose here on earth and to serve or play in the park with our dog or kids, or build things, or go move our bodies, you know, the things that make life worth living. Because we've all heard this one: "Eat to live, not, Live to Eat." And truly, this is what intuitive eating and not dieting gives us, freedom. Because when we're restricting and undernourished, our thoughts will be consumed with food, day in and day out. Our natural bodily instincts go into starvation mode (adaptive thermogenesis) from a prolonged caloric deficit; this will cause instinctually focusing the brain's power and energy towards conservation and finding food. And until the body is fed properly, we cannot have the freedom to eat and move on with our lives.

Food is not used for numbing emotions, escaping responsibilities or frustrations, or satisfying emotional desires and/or disasters. Food is not for when we're bored; it is not a toy. Food is not here to tempt our "willpower" because we've suddenly decided certain foods, portions, and percentages are ideal, and anything outside of our set guidelines is bad.

Food is fuel. Our body does not lie to us when it sends cravings for wholesome macronutrients. You are *not* weak if you eat normally and you give into your body's signals to feed it. Hunger is an instinct. When in famine, we desire more food. That's why we crave carbs when we're on a low-carb diet, why we crave fatty foods when we're on a low-fat diet, or why we crave certain foods when we've deemed them as bad or fattening or toxic or not natural for our species or whatever else we come up with. The more you try to avoid something, the more often it 'suddenly' pops up around you.

I remember I used to be deathly afraid I was pregnant when I started missing my periods or they became irregular. At these times, I noticed more than ever, baby ads on the internet, pregnancy commercials on tv, pregnancy tests in the grocery store, etc. The fact I wanted to avoid and not focus on being pregnant, because I feared it, the more it popped up to haunt me in my life and I started to notice it everywhere around me. Another example is if someone tells you not to look at the color blue in the room, at that moment, you notice everything blue in the room, whereas prior, all the many colors were neutral in your focus.

These examples are in accordance with food restriction. The moment you deem grains, fruit, fats, carbs, bread, butter, cookies, cheese, pizza, etc. as *bad*, you then notice these fear foods more often than ever before. You focus on them and notice them everywhere around you. You think about them more frequently and become obsessed.

Discipline is not a bad thing. Some people just abuse it. It's not even that you lack willpower; if you've been involved and entrapped in all these restrictive diets and have an eating disorder, you have shown to have will power that far surpasses anyone else! You would typically hear the normal non-dieter, person say: "I just don't understand how someone could possibly have an eating disorder, or not eat certain foods, because I just *love eating* and I love "blank" foods too much to stop eating them!"

You may find, as you are getting your intuition back as you hit your 8-month or 1 year mark in recovery, and feel you're rekindling a healthy and fearless relationship with food again... but you still have nagging thoughts that sporadically pop up about how many calories the food you're eating has, or thoughts of if the foods are low-fat, low-carb, if it's "pure," or try to analyze every ingredient in every piece of the take-out you're enjoying with friends. Don't beat yourself up, but be aware of this voice and know when to shut it up or tune it out, so you can carry on with your carefree night out or day to day life.

A good signal to look for when you're "full" is as you're eating and the food no longer tastes as good anymore as it did when you began eating and you stop thinking about food. Also, if you finish what's on your plate and you're still thinking about food, and feel you could eat more and want more, that's a sure sign you should continue eating, until satisfaction. The extreme appetite slows down after weeks or months as you are consistent. If you restrict again, because you want to stay stick thin, or you're fearful of gaining more weight from eating more that your mind's used to, you'll just start the process all over again.

I intend to be vague with everything here, timelines, guidelines, meal plans, when and what to eat and how much, how long recovery lasts, etc. because everyone is so unique, if you haven't got that point yet. Every recovery will look different for each individual, and you may get every symptom in the book and more, while another person hardly gets any. Their recovery symptoms may last a couple weeks or months only, while yours is ongoing for 6 months or for two years. My goal is to be so vague with no flat answers that you'll be forced to think for yourself to answer your own questions. That should be the point of everyone, to take your dependency off someone else, some other guru, coach, or whoever (who's advice isn't even tailored to you) and become independent you can make your own conclusions and decisions based on your needs, desires, likings, biofeedback, etc.

THE ROOT OF YOUR ED

Without having a genetically pre-disposition (because Eating Disorders are sometimes, but not always, mental illnesses that can also be genetic), normal environmental "triggers" for you are not usually "triggers" for someone NOT genetically predisposed. This is why you can take the same dietary information and go to the extremes of a full-blown eating disorder, while someone else who doesn't have the ED genes to "turn on" doesn't take the dietary information that far. If any of the following, caused your eating disorder: *going on a diet, or going through an abusive relationship, experiencing trauma, were told you were "fat" by someone, embarking on a cleanse/detox protocol, or you were abandoned by a loved one,* then everyone who tries or goes through these same things would have an eating disorder too. This is not always the case, (yet, many people do have eating disorders these days; it's just a matter of *to what extent*), which is why these are not always necessarily the "causes" of your eating disorder, just "triggers." And because you are genetically predisposed to having an eating disorder or mental illnesses, the experience(s) just caused you to go into a caloric deficit and trigger the eating disorder gene to switch on.

You could be on the other side of the spectrum and simply be that person who experienced one or multiple reasons I just listed above (i.e., went on a restrictive diet, or cleanse, trauma, bullied or told you were fat, abusive relationships, abandonment, etc.), and because of the caloric deficit you induced as a reaction, both starving your body and brain, you can literally go mental from this and develop a full blown restrictive eating disorder from that point. The eating disorder was just the tool you chose or was the coping mechanism to deal with the pain or trauma or your attempt to control the situation. The physical side effects from dieting can indefinitely lead to mental changes. In these cases, your current eating behaviors exist because something interrupted them, not because normal eating habits were not present for you. This can be changed by sticking through recovery.

Whether you over-eat, or under-eat, both are eating disorders, as you attempt to cope with whatever the root cause was; rather than drugs, alcohol, over-working, or over-exercising, the *food (both under-eating or over-eating of it)*, in these cases, are the substance to help you feel numb, control, avoidance, and/or comfort over the situation.

Regardless of the start of your Eating Disorder, it can be important for the underlying issue of restriction to stop in order to recover.

That's why it's important to realize and identify your triggers, so you can avoid them or know how to manage them when you face them again during recovery and/or in the future after full recovery. Because the eating disorder will be *dormant*, not fully absent, or it might be fully absent for you; it just depends. Don't let your triggers cause you to relapse! This is also why I mention journaling and internal self-work, so you can figure out what the root cause is, if you want to that is; it is unnecessary though. Just keeping the options open!

Nineteen of the thirty-six volunteers for the Minnesota Starvation experiment, almost sixty years later, in 2003, were interviewed as a history project experiment. They admitted to having lingering aftereffects of the experiment sometimes. For many years, they were haunted by a fear that food might be taken away from them again. They remained able not to revert though and still look at the experience as a great and important event in their lives.

*There makes no difference whether starvation is self-induced or forced: when food is scarce, all mental and physical processes become directed towards the search for food, and all other human characteristics-sociability, sex drive, other interests, are subordinate to the fight for survival. Numerous factors contribute to the start of an eating disorder. including genetic predispositions, upbringing, social experiences. and cultural expectations. The most urgent requirement at the start of treatment of anorexia is that weight be regained; understanding the causes of the eating disorder can happen later. (*Psychology Today.com*)*

You honestly just have to LET GO. Let go of the fears, let go of the dogmas, let go of the calorie counting and being an ingredient Nazi when you're just out spending quality time with loved ones or by yourself during you time. It is important to nourish our bodies with wholesome foods and not *only* eat total artificial and chemical laden foods. But there's a point where this should not rule or dictate our lives, our decisions, or take over our thoughts and make us fearful. If you're reading this and know you have disordered eating habits and an unhealthy fear-based relationship with food, know there was a starting point to this all, and the minor changes turned into long-term obsessions, fears, and phobias. We have to come back from this and ultimately try to forget about a lot of the things we learned and came to believe, to regain and restore our intuition.

Journaling is highly encouraged. It is a powerful tool to be expressive and a great therapeutic outlet. Journaling can help you investigate all aspects of yourself that have been brushed under the carpet, suppressed, and forgotten about. It can help you discover the root cause or main trigger that switched on your Eating Disorder. (This can be focused on later in your recovery though.) You can also discover old passions and goals you lost when you started the whole disordered lifestyle. Perhaps, these talents, goals, dreams never got to be expressed or able to flourish, and now, you can have a second chance at creating again! (It's never too late in life to embark on your life's purpose or dreams and share what you offer the world in your own unique way!)

DEFINE YOUR PURPOSE AND IDEA OF SUCCESS

Just like in the *Minnesota Starvation Experiment* in 1946, I too became unnaturally obsessed and all-consumed with food cookbooks, recipes, blogs, social media accounts, nutritional research and talking only on the subject of nutrition, health and healing, unhealthy amounts of exercise, and lost all passion for relationships, life purpose, passion, healthy exercise, hobbies, going to fun events, etc.

There is so much more to live for in life than looking a certain way, getting to a certain weight or BMI, or obsessing on your diet. Life is too short to focus the majority of your energy and brain power on obsessing over your diet and your body image. Once you stop this madness and quit the obsessions, you'll be amazed at how much extra time you have in your life to think about more important and meaningful things in life you were sent here to do. You must work to identify your value beyond your aesthetic, weight, and shape that our culture pushes upon us from the day we're born. There's something bigger for you to focus on, whether it's your career, passion, your purpose, your marriage/partnership, your volunteer work, your art, your dream to travel, whatever. When you make your body your #1 priority, you can't focus on the other important, more meaningful and gratifying things in life.

It's time to pick up a new hobby, because as you go through recovery and succeed at getting over these obsessions around diet and free up time and brain space, you'll be bored and tempted to relapse into old thought patterns. This can happen if you don't fill your time and thoughts with new passions, relationships, and hobbies, or something not focused around food, intense exercise, body appearance, and nutrition. There are so many things you can look into, meet up groups in every town, online courses to take and learn from, books to read with great information and stories, writing a book, volunteering, working, sewing, gardening, cleaning, designing, website design, learn a new language, camping, you get the idea!

Make goals and map out actions you need to take to accomplish it, with goals in place to be excited about and passionate for, it takes your focus off looping thoughts about food and body image all day. When you have friends to hang out with, energy to hike and play sports, play games, dance, fall in love, drink wine, belt out your favorite song lyrics, work on your passions, serve others, communicate about other things than food, and more, your life becomes much more fulfilling, and it takes the place of the obsessive thoughts around dieting, restricting, body degrading, and food. You become so entrenched and involved in your day to day life that is so much fun, you don't have time, or the desire to be that uptight, obsessive, and restrictive anymore. Of course this comes if you are also taking actions to work on your body image so it does not control nor prevent you from going to do these things either. You cannot ignore or suppress negative body image thoughts and think happy thoughts will override the programming — you must actively work to face them, replace them, and overcome them.

Find a purpose larger than yourself and live for it. Living with an eating disorder is selfish, whether our intensions are to be or not. It's just the nature of an eating disorder. When we're caught up worrying about ourself, living by what to eat, what not to eat, what we look like, what others are thinking of us, what we have to prove to others, how much fame we get, how many followers we get, how much weight or muscle we put on or lose, what to do to keep ourself from ever aging (which aging is inevitable, for the best of us) or anything of that nature is only for ourself. But if we can find something to live for, outside of this self-bubble, we will do so much more good for the world and in turn, ourselves. When we become selfless, we can look outside of ourselves and live for something greater, which is more gratifying.

Of course I do not mean become completely selfless and never look out for yourself. Definitely do not do that. This whole recovery thing is supposed to be about your healing and health. The point is, find a balance between you time and self care as well as putting out service to the world. In the end, in order to be able to provide service to the world, you must be in good health and good spirits to be able to bring quality service to the table. If you are not well mentally or physically, how can you in turn show up for the world? You must work on yourself first in order to show up as the best version of yourself for your friends, clients, coach, etc.

"You do not have to know your purpose, in order to live with purpose." -Frank J. Porcaro.

We get caught up with these ideals of what "success" is and see success only as big endeavors, accomplishments, fame, money, having a "perfect" body type, having thousands of followers on social media, etc. We often overlook the simpler things and more important things in life, even day to day, which are the most important! It truly is the little things that count. Without the pieces, you can't have the whole. Without the baby steps, you can't arrive at your destination. Success is a personal interpretation and definition, and it may just change over time as you go through different stages of life; my goals are likely not your goals, and your goals will not be someone else's goals.

Just do what makes you happy, and that, in this moment, is *your* purpose for *this moment.*

That's not to say it's not healthy to have long-term goals, but it's just as equally important, if not more, to enjoy the *process* of *finding* your purpose. Because once you get that "ah-ha!" moment where you may figure out your "purpose," you'll realize, what got you to that moment was the baby steps and the journey itself, and that WAS your purpose all along. Each day you lived, worked, helped your family, was a supportive friend, a helping hand at your church, or a smile in someone's bad day; the research, the trials and errors, the successes and failures, the whole time were each mini purpose's that just led you to an even bigger purpose! And don't think it stops there. We can have many purposes in life, as well, for each chapter in our life. You may master some form of knowledge, experience, or practice, and it's time to share your knowledge now, but then later on, face another trial, master that lesson, which then turns into a new passion, and now, it's time to share and teach this other lesson to others. Passions are influenced, not only by our past life experiences, but also by the issues and people we face, right now, in our current relationships, stresses, and physical and emotional health issues.

The process of success does not happen overnight and will not change overnight. Expecting to find success in instant solutions (instant wealth, instant health, instant healing, relationships, recognition, achievement) sets you up for lifelong disappointment. Success, like learning to walk as a kid, is a process that occurs in tiny *baby* steps. In any endeavor, success indefinitely occurs through steps.

Realize that you do not have to re-create the wheel but see what others have done or seek situations similar to yours; learn the secrets of these other great *students* of life that developed the maturity and passion to succeed. Welcome the uncomfortable moments of "change" and embrace it in your life; stop trying to medicate the unpleasant and unfamiliar feelings with restricting, purging, drugs, alcohol, excessive shopping, excessive exercise, too much internet use, or whatever your choice. The tough and uncomfortable times may be the seeds to your breakthroughs.

Change and success take time. To be and feel successful, you must be able to be honest about your current state, situation, and the things that are important to you; what do you want? What will be the most sustainable for you? What do you really want to do? What gives you the most peace of mind/happiness/passion/love? What do you really want to pursue? What kind of relationships do you want to be involved with?

Never think something is right or wrong all the time, nor be limited to those beliefs; be open to change and always be on the pursuit to what FEELS right to YOU. Things are always changing, progressing; that's the nature of life. Be open to being wrong and being okay with being wrong; this openness allows change and growth! If you are not open to receive change and new information, you'll be the most stagnant human being and miss out on great growth opportunities.

Be okay with humility. Stay humble. We're all wrong or right, in our own minds, so who are you really to say you're right and everyone else is wrong? I'm not claiming what I'm sharing is 100% right for you. I'm just sharing with you what I've learned in my journey, so you can take something from it and add it into your story, making it unique to work for your journey!

Learn how to say NO to what's not serving you in your life anymore. Learn how to be okay with "failure" because if you keep trying each time you fail or feel rejected, you'll get stronger, and the failure will eventually turn into a success. The only way you truly fail is if you accept the fail as your reality or "fate" and you don't keep trying, experimenting, and seeking.

Why not take the risk or another risk? You're not going to get out of this life alive; that is something that is for sure. You might as well follow whatever is tugging at your heart, even if it looks scary and hard! Most chances are, you'll come out of the other side of the risk feeling stronger and more able to take on your goals and life in a better way, feeling more empowered. Stop caring so much and putting so much energy into the distractions that don't matter and are keeping you from your true purpose and values.

"Sometimes, you have to go against everything you 'know' or learned to be 'true' in order to find the answers or 'success' you are seeking." This is something my friend in Hawaii told me, and it changed my life forever; this is my 'light bulb moment' that helped shatter my limiting beliefs and dogmas I'd been painfully following and holding onto for so many years stealing my life and health. These are the words that saved my life. When I took the risk to go against everything I had learned about and believed to be the "truth" for health and healing and fitness and mortality and happiness and everything else, that's when I found what was holding me back. I got a huge slap in the face by reality and what I needed to implement to attain these.

"Whenever we need to make an important decision, it is best to trust our instincts, because reason usually tries to remove us from our dreams saying that the time is not yet right, reason is afraid of defeat, but intuition enjoys life and its challenges." (Paulo Coelho, The Alchemist)

Reason and logic too often get in the way, usually, in the face of fear, of what we truly want to do or to pursue, or 'change' in order for what needs to happen for our benefit. Reason is so afraid of failure, defeat, or rejection. Intuition sees 'problems' as good challenges or times for growth, play, experience, excitement, or expansiveness. You need to have a freedom and abundance based mindset. Not a fearful and scarcity mindset. Ask yourself how you can be accepting and free now. What can you do to help you feel freedom and acceptance now? Not "I have to do this first, and THEN I can feel acceptance and freedom." It needs to come now.

Every time you're saying yes to something that is no longer serving you, you are missing out on something that *would* serve you! Your "self-care" time is needed and just as important as everyone else. Honor yourself and speak YOUR truth. You're not telling people *what to do* or control the world, but just say how you feel, or believe, or speak up against something you don't respect hearing from them.

CLOSE SUPPORT

It's important to have someone around that knows you and your behaviors and has called you on your bullshit, someone who loves you enough to be honest with you. Someone who, even in your depths of your ED, and through all your manipulation and lies to hide your ED, they saw right through it and was that "nagger" who was the most annoying to you and your ED, and who tried to push you to get better when you were still in denial. This person is someone you already have had conflict with during your ED, because they've tried to tell you you need help, or you look way too thin, or say they're worried about you, or tell you you need to eat. You've probably been avoiding this person because of these reasons.

You need them now. You are not a burden to them if you are trying to heal and recover. They love you and want to help, but you were only a burden when you were in denial and they had to watch you suffer and hurt yourself.

You don't want someone easily manipulated into your sob stories, or your lies, or will tell you what you want to hear to avoid conflict. Your ED loves these people, because they support and enable the restrictive ED to flourish and live. You also do not want this person to have any disordered behaviors or mindsets around food, or they can, and will, trigger your ED.

I love and respect my family to pieces, but several have diet mentality behaviors around eating and their body as well (definitely not to my extremes). I found it a big challenge and lesson, whilst still in recovery, not to let these mentalities trigger me back in to restricting or feeling bad about myself. Because I felt huge triggers pop up in my mind every time they made disordered eating or body shaming type remarks around their eating patterns or their body dysmorphia. Examples: how guilty they felt after eating, guilt around eating 'too much,' (when really they were just eating to satisfaction), the unsatisfactory feelings towards how they looked, their weight, or constantly voicing the 'pounds they needed to lose,' or how unhappy they were with the number on the scale, or how they tried to skip meals, or say they don't want to eat later because of how much they just ate, or how they need to go on a diet, or how they need to cut out x, y, or z, or how they needed to detox, you know remarks like these. Don't let anyone hinder your recovery, no matter how tempting.

When you're in recovery, don't think your ED voice and inner critic are going to disappear magically. Nope, they'll be there stronger than ever, fighting to survive, trying to challenge you and your new endeavor. The ED will try to get you to go back, screaming at you, and justifying why you need to restrict, purge, or overexercise again, and why you shouldn't trust yourself or your body's needs. You'll be tempted to go back to old ways, old dogmas, old patterns, and relapse. But if your person who can see this behavior is around to put a stop to it and keep you on track, it will be much harder for the ED voice to get through to you. Think of someone like a parent, which is best, or a partner, a good friend, or a trustworthy person, who truly cares about your wellbeing and are not around for selfish reasons.

If you have absolutely no one around or just no one you feel comfortable recovering around, another option is to check yourself into inpatient care, where you'll give over complete control and be totally hands off everything; you can also seek outpatient care or seek guidance from your trusted doctor.

Another way, many people do it these days (including what I did) is get help and support from people online who run their businesses around recovery; there are plenty of other people, besides me, on the internet to help. I will not sit here and only try to sell you my services, so you just have to find who you resonate most with. If I am that person, then great. I've dedicated much time and effort to make my online course as a great educational and supportive system I highly value. If not, I have faith you'll find what you need!

Depending on how deep in the disordered eating you are, you *may* also have to move back in with your parents, other family, or any other person you really trust will support you (if you haven't done so already, because eating disorders can have a huge impact on our ability to work and function in life). This will help you and get you back on your feet, no matter what age you are.

This book is meant for general advice, something that worked for me and many others, from the research and experience I have. But again, support outside this book, someone you can converse with, learn from, hear insight from, and talk to on email, Skype, phone, in person, group coaching, group forums, support groups, safe and private Facebook groups, etc. is highly recommended.

LEAVE THE BOOK WITH THIS...

Release the expectations of the outcome and the entire process. Become unattached to the results and just do it, one step at a time.

Take ownership by accepting where you are RIGHT NOW in your life. Accept the body you have now, whether in recovery or 20 pounds from when you were a teenager. Accept your self for how you are now, as if your body is your permanent body. Love your body, don't care if you lose or gain weight. Accept it all as it is; stop trying to change everything, stop trying to *do* everything, stop trying to control everything...just try to BE here now and ask what can you do *now* in this moment to get you to where you want to be tomorrow?

With being able to accept where you are now and take ownership over your life, you're not blaming other people for where you've been or where you're at now in your life; you're accepting and owning where you're at in life. With this responsibility taken, no one else holds power over you preventing you from healing and moving forward. There will always be influences and temptations, but you always have a choice to be a 'victim' or a 'victor!' (As Joel Osteen puts it).

This isn't happening TO you. This is happening FOR you! Ask why this happened for you. What lessons have you learned or what can you learn from it? What will you NOW DO with the knowledge you have? What ACTIONS will you take, what sacrifices will you make for your health, body, mind, and life's sake?

Damn The Diets

"What are you willing to give up, to have the life you keep pretending you want?" ~Elizabeth Gilbert.

You CAN do whatever you set your heart and mind to. You WILL succeed. I BELIEVE in your healing. I KNOW you'll get your life and joy back if you take action. You DESERVE health and happiness. You are WORTH the freedom, love, satiety, and sanity.

Don't focus on the damage that's done from your decisions, behaviors, and eating disorder; focus your energy on knowing you still have another chance, and there's always hope for recovery. No matter how far deep you're in, how long you've been suffering, how engrained you are in the habits and beliefs, or how much damage has been done, you can heal, break free, recover, and get on with your life! It's okay to feel upset at the damage created from your disordered eating lifestyle, but you need not dwell in this pool of sorrow forever. Do what you can now, with the knowledge you have, and the opportunity you have now, to make an educated choice for yourself. Know the damage is reversible if you commit and do the work yourself 110%.

Pat yourself on the back for every extra bite you take that is full of fat, full of starch, full of salt, full of sugar, and is not just lettuce and fruit or chicken and asparagus. Be proud of the progress you make at having even just one more body confident thought over body degrading thoughts. Be happy you're on the road to recovery, and you're a step away from heart failure, kidney failure, and any other organ or tissue failure as a result from malnutrition, overtraining, and restrictive eating disorders. Be proud of yourself for where you are now, the food you're feeding yourself now, and for where you're headed.

We may sometimes feel nothing is ever good enough, nor are we good enough, despite our constant efforts of "doing" and the progress and success we *have* indeed achieved. Lacking self-worth is a big contributing factor that fuels these feelings of lack and inadequacy. Feeling we are enough can come from us celebrating and acknowledging our efforts we've already been achieving. Be proud of yourself.

A Tip, Post Script: Re-read this book as often as you need throughout your recovery to keep your anxiety at ease. Read this book again in 6 months, a year, or read it at whatever different stages of your recovery you desire. Each time, you'll get something new and something that resonates with you at that point, rather than what you needed to hear the first time around. What you read in this book that takes only a few days or a couple of weeks, is stuff that happens over months and years. If you read the same book at one point, and then 6 months to a year later, your brain will pick up a totally different message or understanding than it would in the previous different mindset. A year into my recovery, I was still having lightbulb moments and 'ah-ha' moments. I continued to learn new things and 'sprout the seeds of thought' that were once just seedlings (information) planted in my mind (that I wasn't yet ready to hear or implement) from someone or something, months or years prior. I was still re-reading books and forums 10 months and after a year into my recovery to keep me on track so those pesky ED thoughts didn't (and still don't) creep back in, EVER!

FEEDBACK

Hey lovelies, I really appreciate you taking the time to read my book!

Will you take a moment? :)

If this book helped you to gain knowledge, insight, or encouragement to start your recovery journey, then I may ever so humbly ask of you to take a few minutes of your precious time to write your honest review on Amazon or whichever source purchased from!

Your feedback is beyond important; it can help my book reach out to people who may need it!

Thank you :)

~Kayla Rose Kotecki

DamnTheDiets.com

ABOUT THE AU-THOR

I'm a rebel Holistic Nutritionist who's sick of women and men struggling and suffering from restrictive eating disorders caused by unrealistic and unsustainable diet culture and beauty standard demands.

I want to help guid people back from the mental and physical damage and programming that is done from the media, modern society, the health and fitness industry, and other various popular "fad" diet trends.

I spent sleepless nights, because all I could think about was developing quality, real, authentic content, such as this book, my courses, and my business around sharing this message to help spread awareness and help others.

I put everything I know and all my efforts I had into this stuff. All I want and hope for is to help someone with similar struggles that I faced whilst in my restrictive eating disorder shenanigans, feeling like death, but not knowing what to do or how to begin recovery.

Allow me to help you! :)

Follow Me On:

Instagram: @damnthediets

Youtube: Kayla Rose Kotecki

Facebook: Kayla Rose Kotecki

Blog: damnthediets.com/blog

ACKNOWLEDGMENTS

I'll try to keep this short 'n sweet.. the take away here is that I'm beyond appreciative for these humans.

Mum - Pops - Grams - Sis - Bro

Thank you for always supporting me with my extreme endeavors, never giving up on me, and loving me unconditionally no matter what crazy phase or escapade I was embarking on. Thank you for encouraging me to follow my passions and live true to myself, and not try to pressure or mold me into something other than that. Thank you for being good friends as well as loving family. And thank you for helping to make my dreams, my reality. I couldn't have done it without any of you, and will be forever grateful for each one of you in a unique way. You guys each deserve a book on its own about your greatness. ;)

Cover Photo Credit: Alexandria Bailey